DETROIT'S COLD WAR

THE WORKING CLASS IN AMERICAN HISTORY

Editorial Advisors
James R. Barrett
Alice Kessler-Harris
Nelson Lichtenstein
David Montgomery

A list of books in the series
appears at the end of this book.

DETROIT'S COLD WAR

The Origins
of Postwar
Conservatism

COLLEEN DOODY

**UNIVERSITY OF
ILLINOIS PRESS**
Urbana, Chicago, and Springfield

First Illinois paperback, 2017
© 2013 by the Board of Trustees
of the University of Illinois
All rights reserved
1 2 3 4 5 C P 5 4 3 2 1
∞ This book is printed on acid-free paper.

The Library of Congress cataloged the cloth edition as follows:
Doody, Colleen.
Detroit's Cold War : the origins of postwar conservatism / Colleen Doody.
   p.   cm. — (The working class in American history)
Includes bibliographical references and index.
ISBN 978-0-252-03727-6 (cloth : acid-free paper)
1. Detroit (Mich.)—Politics and government—20th century.
2. Detroit (Mich.)—Social conditions—20th century.
3. Cold War—Social aspects—Michigan—Detroit—History.
4. Conservatism—Michigan—Detroit—History—20th century.
5. Anti-communist movements—Michigan—Detroit—History—20th century.
6. Working class—Michigan—Detroit—History—20th century.
7. Catholics—Political activity—Michigan—Detroit—History—20th century.
8. Businessmen—Political activity—Michigan—Detroit—History—20th century.
9. Political culture—Political activity—Michigan—Detroit—History—20th century.
I. Title.
F574.D457D66   2012
977.4'34043—dc23   2012017781

PAPERBACK ISBN 978-0-252-08310-5

CONTENTS

ACKNOWLEDGMENTS

This manuscript marks the end of a long and intellectually arduous process. It began as a work on American anti-Communism during the early Cold War. However, at the suggestion of the editors of the Working Class in America series at University of Illinois Press, I rewrote the book to focus instead on the roots of twentieth-century American conservatism. Their suggestion made a great deal of sense at this particular political moment. With the rise of the Tea Party, the United States is once again in the midst of a conservative revival. Many of the ideas contemporary conservatives raise will be quite familiar to readers of this book. I hope that this work will help make sense of the current rhetoric, with its obsession with Socialism and Communism having been pulled directly from the Cold War.

I have been enormously fortunate to work with Nelson Lichtenstein throughout the writing process. Nelson is without a doubt one of the most intellectually generous mentors a writer could have. He has read this work in countless iterations and has always been insightful and encouraging. I cannot thank him enough. During my years at University of Virginia, I was also privileged enough to work with Melvyn Leffler, whose intellect and insight profoundly shaped my work. No academic could have asked for better models than these two scholars.

At DePaul University, I have been lucky enough to have wonderful colleagues in the History Department who give me both the occasional pep talk and motivational kick. Lisa Sigel in particular has read and reread various revisions of this work, always providing me with enormously helpful guidance. I am forever grateful for all her insights and support. I also benefitted from grants from DePaul's University Research Council, which provided me with much needed research leave as well as funding to cover copyediting and indexing.

One of the great advantages of working in Chicago is having access to an incredible community of scholars. I was able to present my chapter on labor to the Newberry Seminar in Labor History. Thanks to Martha Biondi and Stephen Meyer for their insightful comments. I'm especially grateful that Stephen Meyer told me about the Likert papers at the Bentley Library, University of Michigan. In addition to the Newberry, I was lucky enough to participate in the North American Religions Workshop at Northwestern University. Robert Orsi and the other participants of the workshop read my chapter on Catholic anti-Communism and provided me with greatly helpful suggestions.

I'd also like to thank Laurie Matheson of the University of Illinois Press, the anonymous readers, and the editorial advisors of the Working Class in American History series, particularly Jim Barrett. They all provided critical feedback and suggestions that have made this a better project overall.

Finally, I would like to thank Bridget, my wonderful and talented partner who gave me moral and intellectual support throughout this project. And I thank my mother, who passed away before this project was completed. She nurtured my curiosity from the very beginning, and I owe her an incredible debt of gratitude for encouraging my love of history.

DETROIT'S COLD WAR

INTRODUCTION

One evening during the late 1940s, a Catholic housewife on the east side of Detroit knocked on the doors of the eighteen families on her block. This woman had decided that she could no longer stand idly by while Communism threatened the United States and the Catholic world. Vowing to fight godless Marxism with prayer, she asked all the families on her block to gather together once a week to pray the Rosary for the conversion of Russia. Her neighbors responded enthusiastically: sixteen of the families participated. Kneeling in one family's living room, clutching their Rosary beads, they implored the Virgin Mary to destroy Communism and lead the United States away from secularism. By 1952, these eastside families were joined by thousands of other Detroit-area Catholics who hoped and prayed that Mary would vanquish the "modern-day anti-Christ"—the Communists.[1]

In a very different part of Detroit just a few years after the housewife began her Rosary group, B. E. Hutchinson, the chairman of the finance committee at Chrysler, asked why Socialism and Communism were so popular. He speculated, "Heretical political and economic ideas are at once the more appealing and the more insidious when presented under the guise of a New Deal, a Fair Deal or a Welfare State." He urged his listeners to resist, not only because such ideologies did not work well, but also because "Capitalism is compatible with the dignity and liberty of the individual man, which *they* are not."[2]

Both the anonymous Catholic housewife and B. E. Hutchinson lived in the years before a coherent conservative movement existed, yet they each expressed some of the core ideas of late-twentieth-century conservatism—embrace of religious traditionalism, celebration of laissez-faire capitalism, hostility toward big-government liberalism, and opposition to Communism.[3] As many scholars of American conservatism have pointed out, these ideals were not necessarily smoothly compatible. Who knows, for example, if a housewife from one of the most heavily working-class, industrial areas of Detroit would agree with an executive of one of the largest corporations in the country in his enthusiastic celebration of unregulated capitalism. Yet, their ideologies shared one key component: anti-Communism. For both the Catholic housewife and the laissez-faire businessman, their opposition to Communism was much more than fear of the strategic power of the Soviet Union. Instead, their hostility to Communism grew out of their larger critique of American society. *Detroit's Cold War* explores the beginnings of post–World War II popular conservatism, particularly the glue that held this disparate movement together: anti-Communism.

Ronald Reagan's victory in 1980 and the rise of the conservative movement flummoxed scholars, many of whom viewed the twentieth century through the lens of the liberal consensus. According to this theory, which was first articulated in the years shortly after World War II, Far Left and Far Right ideologies had disappeared in the United States. In their place, according to historians like John Higham, a broad agreement existed throughout society on questions of political economy and class relations. American capitalism was so productive and so successful at spreading affluence that struggles over class inequality had disappeared. Any groups that challenged this consensus, according to these consensus scholars, did so out of psychological need rather than economic interest. As Lionel Trilling snidely asserted, by the 1950s, liberalism was the nation's "sole intellectual tradition" because there were "no conservative or reactionary ideas in general circulation." The "conservative impulse" did not express itself "in ideas but only in action or in irritable mental gestures which seek to resemble ideas."[4] Subsequent scholarship was perhaps less dismissive. Nevertheless, as one prominent scholar of American politics noted in the mid-1990s, "Most historians have told the story of twentieth-century American political and cultural development by emphasizing the triumph of the progressive-liberal state and of the modern, cosmopolitan sensibility that has accompanied and to a large degree supported it."[5]

Some of the earliest researchers who attempted to explain the rise of conservatism in the 1980s argued that consensus disappeared in the 1960s and 1970s as the nation was split apart by issues of race, economics, and morality. According to scholars like Jonathan Rieder, Dan Carter, and Thomas and Mary Edsall, antipoverty and affirmative-action programs angered northern and southern white workers, who complained of reverse discrimination and who turned against the liberals in the federal government who had thrown their support behind the civil rights movement. Radicals who protested against the American government by burning flags or challenging police angered white workers, who embraced what they saw as traditional moral values of patriotism and respect for authority. White workers, who had been the backbone of New Deal liberalism, began to abandon their erstwhile liberal allies. This was especially true of the formerly solidly Democratic south. White southerners first supported George Wallace and Richard Nixon, and they became key to Ronald Reagan's 1980 victory.

More recently, scholars have challenged this thesis. On the one hand, some historians have argued that the South was no different than the North, Midwest, or West: race played a key role in the rise of conservatism. Nor did this challenge only exist among workers. Southern suburbanites, for example, challenged school desegregation and rallied around the concept of homeowner's rights to maintain their solidly white schools and communities.[6] Other scholars have pushed the timeline back well before the 1960s and have found challenges to the liberal consensus before the 1960s. Thomas Sugrue, for example, found homeowners groups in Detroit who fought neighborhood desegregation and attempts to build public housing in the years immediately after World War II.[7] Other scholars have explained the rise of conservatism by exploring issues other than race. Lisa McGirr argued that Orange County, California housewives, driven by their sense that the nation was endangered by liberal "collectivism," formed a conservative grassroots political movement that predated the racial struggles of the 1960s.[8] Kim Phillips-Fein and Elizabeth Shermer explored the crucial role economics played as businessmen both popularized a libertarian antiregulation, antiunion, and antitaxation philosophy and crafted a movement designed to spread these ideas.[9] Still other historians have explored the role religion, particularly evangelicalism, played in creating a conservative movement. Allan Lichtman argued that modern conservatism developed out of a "widespread concern that pluralistic, cosmopolitan forces threatened America's national identity," which was based on a view that the United States was a white, Protestant nation.[10] Despite their differences, all of these scholars reject the idea that a consensus existed in the mid-twentieth century or that this consensus shattered in response to the civil rights and antiwar movements. Instead, they argued that New Deal liberalism was always contested and that conservatism was far more powerful than earlier generations of historians recognized.

This work builds upon this recent scholarship on conservatism, and I bring their insights to bear on the debate on the nature of early Cold War domestic politics. I argue that the key elements of twentieth-century conservatism— antipathy toward big government, embrace of religious traditionalism, celebration of laissez-faire capitalism, and militant anti-Communism—arose during the 1940s and 1950s out of opposition to the legacy of the New Deal and its modernizing, centralizing, and secularizing ethos.[11] During the postwar period, some Americans formulated a critique of the activist state and pluralist culture that developed during the 1930s; in the process, they helped create a conservative ideology.[12] Although a conservative movement did not cohere until the late 1950s when William F. Buckley Jr. created the *National Review*, and although it remained relatively small until the 1970s and 1980s, the ideas that became central to this movement developed at a grassroots level much earlier.

This project examines a specific urban center and grounds its conception of politics in the daily decisions of a wide variety of individuals rather than on the actions of political elites. The focus on Detroit is central to this project and to a larger understanding of conservatism in America. Unlike Orange County, which was the subject of Lisa McGirr's excellent book, Detroit was home to powerful liberal institutions like the UAW and the NAACP. As historian Julian Zeilzer argued in his review of the literature on American conservatism, recent historians have too often overemphasized the contested and fragmented nature of New Deal liberalism during the postwar period. Zeilzer has called upon historians to explore how "conservatism unfolded in a dialectical fashion with liberalism rather than as a replacement *to* liberalism."[13] This is exactly what occurred in Detroit during the 1940s and 1950s. Detroit was the nexus of labor and industry in the postwar world and was thus a crucial site where the struggle to define the nature of postwar politics and culture was fought.

Many of the key ideas we associate with contemporary conservatism were articulated in debates over Communism and anti-Communism. In Cold War Detroit, opposition to Communism was expressed in local politics, local unions, major corporations, and neighborhood churches. My examination of Detroit's social and political fabric demonstrates that domestic anti-Communism arose out of tensions within American society and politics. Fear of the Soviet Union clearly played a role in shaping and strengthening this movement. However, domestic anti-Communism emerged organically from American society and the problems that fragmented the nation. Rather than seeing anti-Communism as a political moment that stood antithetical to broader cultural currents, this monograph demonstrates that anti-Communism emerged from the central conflicts that defined American society and culture in the postwar world. Many of these conflicts would ultimately lead some Detroiters to embrace a conservative ideology.

Detroit, the fourth largest city in the nation, encapsulated all the tensions and conflicts of industrial America at mid-century. From the vantage point of the early twenty-first century, Detroit might seem like an odd focus for a local study that purports to explore the crucial issues of American politics and culture. But in the mid-twentieth century, Detroit was the symbol of American manufacturing prowess at a time when the United States led the world in industrial production. Detroit's factories built the quintessential product of the consumer republic—the automobile. General Motors and Ford, the largest and most innovative corporations in the country, dominated the city's economy. Some of the most pioneering labor leaders in the nation headed Detroit's unions at a time when labor's strength was approaching its twentieth-century peak.

Detroit was also a place where both Communists and anti-Communists were quite active. In 1947, the city had the third largest Communist Party organization in the United States, with almost seventy cells and fifteen hundred members. In response to the party's power, Detroit voters passed a charter amendment to establish a city loyalty board and make membership in any subversive organization grounds for dismissal from any city job in 1949. Detroit became one of the first cities in the country to create its own loyalty program, which investigated all municipal workers. Both successful candidates in the 1945 mayoral election and the 1946 gubernatorial election won on explicitly anti-Communist platforms. Detroit thus provides an excellent site both to explore the postwar red scare and to consider how domestic tensions created the nascent conservative ideology.[14]

Each chapter in this book examines a particular subject central to the development of conservatism. My study begins with some background on New Deal Detroit in order to provide context for the following chapters. The book then explores the two largest issues that confronted the city's electorate at the end of World War II—labor and race. Chapter 2 demonstrates that local politics in Detroit was roiled by a debate over the power of labor and the expansion of the New Deal state. Labor's size and influence grew rapidly during the New Deal and the war. Despite the fact that Detroit was the most heavily unionized city in the nation, anti-CIO candidates won political office in some crucial elections by linking labor to the Communist Party. While such red baiting was fairly conventional behavior, this language resonated with voters during the mid-1940s who feared labor's strength and chafed against wartime government regulations. In response to their defeats, labor leaders battled to determine the role labor would play in the postwar world while also debating the role Communists and their supporters would play in labor's ranks.

Chapter 3 extends this argument and demonstrates that anti-Communism became a means to debate the proper role of government on the issue of race rights. Liberals and their leftist allies supported the wartime New Deal's vision of an expanded role for government in both fair housing and fair employment for African Americans. They embraced the inclusive, democratic nationalism of the New Deal.[15] Opponents of this view argued that racial advances would come at the expense of white workers and homeowners. These groups supported a far more limited conception of the New Deal, one that shied away from racial equality while providing federal support for white homeownership. They often equated racial egalitarianism with Socialism and Communism. This association was not entirely far fetched—the Communist Party was at the forefront in the fight for race rights during the 1930s. The conflation of the two ideologies served as political fodder for anti–New Deal activism and rhetoric. In response both to right-wing opposition and to Communist activities, liberals turned against the radical left during the postwar period. Liberals argued that they, not the Communists, were the legitimate spokespeople in the fight to improve the legal and social status of African Americans. They contended that Communists acted in the interest of the party and opportunistically used African Americans to further the party's goals. When their aims no longer agreed with the objectives of African Americans, the party abandoned the fight for civil rights.[16] By the end of these first two chapters, we can see how various Detroiters began to articulate an antistatist and anti-Communist ideology that was central to conservatism.

After exploring two major issues that led to the development of conservative ideology, the focus shifts to two important groups that were central to conservatism—Catholics and businessmen. Chapter 4 explores the roots of Catholic conservatism, which developed out of fears that the United States was becoming Godless. The great transformation wrought by the New Deal challenged organized religion in profound ways. Government during the economic collapse of the 1930s stepped in to solve the problems that religious charities could not. From the perspective of numerous workers, the New Deal had saved the nation. The men and women who built the New Deal and developed the CIO were secular liberals, socialists, and even Communists. They advocated policies that looked a great deal like Socialism to many Americans. This created tension in places like Detroit, which, like other northern industrial cities, had a large and devout Catholic community. Catholics made up between 20 percent and 70 percent of the population of the postwar urban industrial north. The Detroit archdiocese, which covered the city and surrounding area, was home to more than one million members, 70 percent of whom attended Mass at least once a week during the 1950s.[17] The industrial working class in particular was both heavily Catholic and Democratic. The New Deal was not hostile to religion, but it did in effect encourage Americans to look to government rather than organized religion to solve the nation's problems. The New Deal also provided openings for radicals to influence major public and private organizations. As a result, many Catholics worried that the increased popularity of secular organizations and ideas endangered the nation and the Western world. Catholics challenged the primacy of secularism and sought to reassert traditional, hierarchical Catholic values even as they worked in modern corporations and lived in modern suburbs.

Since their target was secularism, Catholics often focused on infusing their cultural values into the public sphere. Their weapon of choice was the supernatural, intercessory powers of the Virgin Mary and the Rosary. The idea that mid-twentieth-century Americans living in one of the most industrially advanced cities in the nation would choose to fight Communism with the Rosary and the Virgin Mary demonstrates the way that anti-Communism could emerge organically from people's beliefs. It also illustrates how Catholics configured a conservative ideology that was communitarian and family oriented rather than one based on ideas of personal liberty against state control. But the chapter also illustrates how the anti-Communism that was central to postwar Catholicism provided conservative Catholics with a powerful issue they shared with other conservatives.

Chapter 5 on the Detroit business community focuses on their opposition to the growth of the government. These men made little distinction between the New Deal, Socialism, and Communism. The former, they argued, would ultimately lead to the latter. As a result, Detroit businessmen during the late 1940s and 1950s carried out a campaign to check state power. They targeted labor, particularly the UAW, in this fight because they rightly saw the union as one of the greatest advocates of an expanded welfare state. Like other conservatives, these men were anti-Communists. However, they spent little time discussing the Kremlin or the American Communist Party when they warned against the collectivist threat. Their hostility to Communism was inextricably linked to their perception that free enterprise, as they understood it, was threatened by an expanding welfare state. For most Detroit businessmen, the face of collectivism was UAW President Walter Reuther and Democratic Michigan Governor G. Mennan Williams. Corporate managers discussed such issues as social security, unemployment insurance, and peacetime price controls, all measures that most executives saw as part of the "march toward socialism or collectivism" and that labor-liberals believed were key to creating a modern welfare state.

Together, these chapters explore the texture of society as it developed a new ideological framework. While it pays attention to the rhetoric of conservatism, this book is not a discourse analysis. This work, in contrast, analyzes the political formation of diverse communities at a critical point in American history. Some readers might argue that much of this conservative rhetoric was in fact cynical red baiting designed to silence the left. This was certainly what Communists of the period claimed. Merely repeating their critique does little more than reiterate the agitprop of a period. In each chapter of this book, the development of conservatism is a foregone conclusion. During the 1940s and 1950s, it was not. Instead, conservatism was an emerging belief system that allowed people to mobilize around specific issues. We now know the effect of conservative, particularly anti-Communist, rhetoric, but we should not confuse the consequences with the intent. The red scare did in fact silence the Old Left. That result does not mean that the proponents of conservatism didn't truly believe their stated fears about labor power, racial equality, growing secularism, or the developing welfare state.

CHAPTER ONE

New Deal Detroit, Communism, and Anti-Communism

Anti-Communism, which became a key part of modern conservative ideology, was a central component in postwar political culture. In order to understand Cold War anti-Communism in Detroit, it is important to provide some context on the city of Detroit, New Deal labor, and the Communist Party. As late as 1900, fewer than three hundred thousand people lived in Detroit. However, mass production of the automobile remade the city. By 1920, as a result of the huge demand for labor in the auto plants, Detroit's population surged to 993,675, and the city became the fourth largest in the nation. This expansion meant that most Detroiters were newcomers. Two-thirds of the city's residents in 1920 were either foreign born or the children of immigrants.[1]

Detroit during this period was known as a staunch antiunion, open-shop town largely controlled by the auto industry. The Employers' Association of Detroit proudly dubbed it the "Capital of Industrial Freedom." Even as late as 1928, few of the almost three hundred thousand automobile workers in the Detroit area belonged to a union.[2] Detroit was a "total industrial landscape" whose geography and economy were dominated by massive automobile plants as well as hundreds of small auto parts factories.[3]

However, during the New Deal, industrial unions, especially the UAW, developed relatively rapidly as workers eagerly seized the promise of industrial democracy offered by the Roosevelt administration. The Wagner Act (1935) promised federal protection for the rights of workers to organize unions of their own choosing and to bargain collectively with management. As a result, the newly formed CIO was able to unionize industrial workers in some of the largest, most antiunion manufacturers in the country. Once Roosevelt signed the Wagner Act, laborers all over the industrial Midwest flocked to unions to protect themselves from autocratic employers. In Detroit, General

Motors, the largest corporation in the country, signed a contract with the new UAW-CIO in 1937 after a lengthy sit-down strike. Chrysler, Ford, and the smaller auto companies ultimately followed suit after protracted battles between organizers and management. By 1939, the UAW's national membership reached 165,000.[4]

During World War II, the city experienced both another population leap and a huge increase in union membership as hundreds of thousands of black and white southern migrants poured into Detroit to fill the jobs offered in the Arsenal of Democracy's flourishing plants. While Detroit's total population grew to 1,850,000 in 1950, the African American community more than doubled, from 120,000 in 1930 to 300,000 in 1950. A large percentage of this total population belonged to a union. By 1945, the CIO had 350,000 members in the city, while the AFL had 100,000.[5]

Detroit in the 1940s was thus a boomtown confronted with enormous social and political change. Most Detroit residents had lived there for no more than a generation. The city's political and economic elites struggled to control these newcomers. The migrants themselves fought to assert their rights, which often conflicted with the rights of others. As a result of the growth of both its population and its labor movement, Detroit, a formerly largely white, open-shop town, became the most heavily unionized city in the nation with one of the largest African American populations outside of the South.

Many of the same factors that led to Detroit's population changes also led to the expansion of the city's Communist Party. As the city's auto industry developed during the 1920s, members of the party struggled to organize Detroit's working class. During the Depression, Communists successfully mobilized workers who had lost their jobs during the economic crisis. In March 1930, Communist parties around the world led massive unemployment demonstrations, including one in downtown Detroit that numbered between fifty thousand and one hundred thousand. Party members created more than twenty Detroit-area Unemployed Councils, which helped move evicted families back into their homes. In 1932, these Unemployed Councils and prominent local Communists staged a protest through Detroit to Ford's River Rouge plant in Dearborn to demand food and jobs. Roughly three thousand unemployed workers marched until Dearborn police halted them at the city line. When the marchers refused to turn back, the police used tear gas on them. Hand-to-hand fighting broke out between marchers and the police. As the situation spiraled out of control, the police opened fire on the demonstrators and killed three unemployed workers and one leader of the Young Communists. As one prominent historian of Detroit labor pointed out, "The Ford Hunger march, thanks to the overreaction of the Dearborn police . . . made the Communist party a significant political force in the new wave of radicalism sweeping the auto industry."[6] The march also helped the local party grow. According to the *Daily Worker*, Detroit had the largest Communist Party in the country during the early 1930s.

The Communist Party continued to expand during the 1930s because a small but dedicated cadre played a crucial role in organizing industrial unions, including the UAW. Party members' skill and bravery convinced others to join. One Detroit worker explained that he enlisted in the party during the 1930s because he "saw that the Communists were the strongest force of recruiting union members. They dared everything and we had to have the sort of wildness they generated."[7] Communists helped lead the UAW's sit-down strike that led to the union's first contract with GM. Wyndham Mortimer, a party member and UAW vice president, later claimed that "the main strategy of the sit-down strike itself was conducted by the Communists."[8] As a result of their organizing, Communists in the auto industry, according to a prominent labor historian, "gained for themselves a reputation as superb organizers, hard-working unionists who could lead strikes."[9] Their talents convinced non-Communist labor leaders to tolerate Communist activity in the nascent Congress of Industrial Organizations (CIO).[10] As anti-Communist CIO president John Lewis famously said about the wisdom of permitting party members to play such a prominent role, "Who gets the bird, the hunter or the dog?"[11]

For their part, Communist cadre entered the new industrial labor movement as part of a worldwide Popular Front strategy. The rise of European fascist movements during the early 1930s led the Seventh Congress of the Communist International to encourage party members throughout the world to cooperate with antifascist social democrats. In the United States, this Popular Front strategy led the Communist Party to support the New Deal and the newly emerging industrial unions of the CIO. By the late 1930s, Communists and their supporters held influential leadership positions in the UAW. Party membership reached roughly 2,600 in Michigan and between 50,000 and 75,000 nationwide.[12]

The Communist Party in Detroit also received support from many African Americans, not only because of their organizing around labor and unemployment issues during the Depression but also because they were in the forefront of the fight for civil rights during the 1930s and 1940s. This was a stance that few other political organizations were willing to adopt. Beginning in 1928, the American Communist Party began recruiting blacks into the fold; Communists achieved some notable success, particularly during the battle to unionize the auto, steel, and packinghouse industries. During and after World War II, Communists had a prominent political profile in Detroit through two Popular Front civil rights organizations, the Civil Rights Congress (CRC) and the National Negro Congress (NNC).[13] The interracial CRC focused on defending democratic rights, and it played a key role during the late 1940s in campaigns for the Martinsville Seven, Willie McGee, and other victims of racist justice.[14] The NNC was a black-led organization within the trade-union movement that worked for fair employment practices through direct and political action. Both the CRC and the NNC drew much of their black membership from Local 600, the enormous, multiracial local from Ford's River Rouge plant.

Pre–Cold War Anti-Communism in Detroit

Anti-Communism and antiradicalism had a long history in Detroit. The Ku Klux Klan flourished briefly in the mid-1920s in response to the influx of immigrants and African Americans into Detroit. The Black Legion, an organization that purportedly helped southern white migrants find jobs, had a membership of roughly one hundred thousand in Michigan and Ohio during the mid-1930s. The legion developed connections with corporate interests, local police, and some Republican groups. Claiming that they wanted only "to stamp out communism," legion members beat union and Communist activists, bombed or burned their homes, and were implicated in murder.[15] As in other industrial communities, Detroit industrialists used red baiting to silence radicals and quash nascent unionism.

The crisis of the Depression fundamentally changed anti-Communism in Detroit. The economic collapse of the early 1930s seemingly challenged capitalism and led many Americans to turn to radical ideologies to solve the problems of mass unemployment and widespread hunger. As a result, Detroit's business elites suddenly found their authority contested. Ford, the symbol of the 1920s mass-production economy, fired 91,000 workers between 1929 and 1931, yet they continued to assert, "These are the best times we ever had."[16] The Communist Party exploited the collapse of capitalist authority. Local elites thus reacted with horror when Communists led mass protests in the city. The massive Communist-led march in 1930 brought a congressional committee, led by Congressman Hamilton Fish, to the city to investigate subversives. They heard the police chief of Flint, Michigan, complain that Detroit Communists had traveled to his city to initiate a major strike. Communists, he complained, were moving around the state "to create trouble and to disaffect people."[17] The local Union League of

Michigan, a Republican organization filled with industrialists and bankers, began its own investigation. Both the Union League and the Fish committee called for laws to exclude and deport Communist aliens, denaturalize foreign-born Communists, and outlaw the Communist Party. The Union League also called on the state of Michigan to register aliens. Although no meaningful legislation resulted from these investigations, anti-Communists continued their battle against the increasingly prominent Communist Party. Immediately after the 1932 Ford hunger march, Harry Toy, the local prosecutor, claimed that he had "evidence of criminal syndicalism," and he stated that his investigators had found no evidence that the march was a hunger or unemployment protest. Rather than criticizing the police for shooting protestors, Toy called on the grand jury to return indictments on the syndicalism charge. Local police raided the headquarters of various groups and arrested thirty-five radicals. Anti-Communism thus developed in Detroit during the early 1930s in response to Communist Party demonstrations. Undoubtedly, local elites feared that high unemployment and starvation weakened their status and strengthened the appeal of radicalism. However, rather than seeing radical protests as logical complaints against the economic situation, anti-Communists ignored the marchers' grievances and viewed the demonstrators as alien subversives bent on overthrowing the government.[18]

The New Deal further threatened the hegemony of business elites, particularly since the New Deal's support for labor led to a boom in union membership. While federal protections certainly helped organized labor during the 1930s, the CIO could not have grown without the herculean efforts of union organizers. These men came from a variety of political backgrounds, including from the Communist Party. The presence of party members made the nascent union movement vulnerable to red baiting, which came from all sides. In response to the GM sit-down strike in 1937, for example, Detroit Bishop Michael J. Gallagher claimed that there was "Soviet planning behind it."[19]

As the labor movement grew stronger and as New Dealers became progressively more associated with labor, anti-Communism changed. The New Deal's critics, emboldened by both Roosevelt's failed court-packing scheme and the economic downturn of 1937, increasingly directed their venom against prolabor and pro–New Deal politicians by equating New Deal policies with Communism. In 1937, unionists in a number of industrial cities, including Detroit, ran for local offices in an attempt to wrest political control away from corporate-dominated local governments. Their recent organizing success led them to believe that they could translate union power into political influence. In response to the labor ticket's success in the Detroit primary, the *Detroit Free Press* encouraged voters to remind labor that "this city belongs to the people who live and work in it, and not to Mr. [John L.] Lewis. Let us keep it that way."[20] Mayoral candidate Richard Reading, running against a New Deal Democrat who had the CIO's support, claimed that a victory for his opponent would give Communists control over Detroit's government. The largest voter turnout in the city's history put Reading in office and defeated all of the labor candidates. Although the labor slate won almost twice as many votes as any previous left-wing ticket in Detroit, a majority of Detroit citizens rejected what they perceived as the New Deal's attempt to strengthen labor and centralize power.

Likewise, when Frank Murphy, Michigan's pro–New Deal Democratic governor, ran for reelection in 1938, he faced a barrage of red baiting. Murphy played a crucial role during the 1937 General Motors conflict when he refused to send in troops to break the strike. Republican Harry S. Toy criticized Murphy for failing to "protect honest labor from communists." When the newly created House Un-American Activities Committee (HUAC) visited Detroit in October 1938 to conduct hearings on Communists in the labor movement, Murphy quickly became the target. The Detroit police superintendent claimed that Communists were responsible for 75 percent of recent Detroit area strikes, and he blamed Murphy for encouraging strikers. According to an American Legion authority on subversive activities, Michigan was "one of the most communistically contaminated states in the Union." Despite the fact that President Roosevelt skewered the Dies Committee for attempting to influence an election, Michigan voters rejected Murphy and elected Republican majorities to both houses of the state legislature. In both the 1937 and 1938 elections, candidates who successfully equated Communism with the New Deal and labor power defeated their opponents.[21]

The presence of Communist organizers within the CIO also led to an increase in anti-Communism within the labor movement. An anti-Communist faction developed in the UAW during the late 1930s and coalesced around UAW President Homer Martin. Martin, a former Baptist minister from Kansas City, headed an ethnically and religiously diverse coalition of semi-skilled, native-born, white southern migrants as well as Catholic supporters of Father Charles Coughlin. As Steve Fraser has written, "Martin's followers felt a deep antipathy toward the more secular, cosmopolitan, racially mixed, and often anticlerical, even irreligious, milieu assembled under the radical leaderships" of the Socialists and Communists.[22] Martin quickly found himself enmeshed in a faction fight with the UAW left, led by Communist Wyndham Mortimer. In order to defeat his opponents, Martin brought Jay Lovestone into the union in 1937 to help him purge party members from the union's executive committee. Lovestone was a former Communist who turned against the party after Stalin defeated Nikolai Bukharin for control of the Soviet Communist Party. He began publicly criticizing Stalin's government, which Lovestone characterized as a "bureaucratic clique which is trying to perpetuate itself by brute force, barbaric terror, blackest frame up, and wanton blood spilling." The former party member now urged workers everywhere to destroy this "savage regime unworthy of a free working class and a socialist state."[23]

Lovestone quickly set out to solidify Martin's hold on the UAW's executive committee by moving prominent leftists, including Wyndham Mortimer and Victor Reuther, out of positions of power while creating alliances with non-Communist UAW leaders, particularly Richard Frankensteen. Frankensteen, a popular nonideological and opportunistic leader in the union, allied himself with Martin in exchange for the plum job as head of the Ford organizing campaign. Martin's position at the head of the UAW appeared increasingly secure.[24]

However, Martin's incompetence and autocratic tendencies threatened to destroy the still-fragile young union. His anti-Communist campaign sidelined many of the UAW's most effective organizers. His negotiated agreement with General Motors in August 1937 infuriated many GM workers, who rejected the settlement. In response, the UAW president imposed a new agreement on the GM workers and refused to submit the contract to either the union's executive board or the GM locals. Confronted with criticism and conflict on all sides, Martin purged five of his opponents from the board. Faced with the very real possibility that the union might collapse into chaos, two rival union factions—the Communists and the non-Communist radicals, led by Walter and Victor Reuther—created an alliance against Martin. This coalition was an unstable one, as Socialists and their allies complained of the Communist Party's desire to capture control of the union. However, prominent anti-Communist CIO leaders such as Sidney Hillman and Philip Murray patched over differences within this alliance until they could push Homer Martin out of office. They feared that Martin's impulsiveness could destroy the UAW and thus severely weaken the CIO. In 1939, Martin led about seventeen thousand of his followers out of the CIO and created the UAW-AFL.[25] However, this rump union failed to displace the UAW-CIO, which repeatedly defeated its new rival in NLRB elections during 1939 and 1940. The fragile alliance of Socialists and Communists remained together because both UAW and CIO anti-Communist leaders decided that Martin was a far greater threat to industrial unionism than were the Communists. The 1937–38 red scare in the UAW thus proved brief. It would not be until these non-Communist union leaders believed that the Communist presence in the CIO threatened to destroy their unions that they would purge the party.[26]

The AFL in Detroit

The American Federation of Labor (AFL) eagerly welcomed Homer Martin and his anti-Communist UAW into the fold because Martin confirmed the AFL's long-standing view that Communists dominated the CIO. The federation, whose history of anti-Communism stretched back to the Bolshevik revolution, regularly (and often accurately) accused CIO unions of Communist domination throughout the 1930s. AFL vice president Frank Duffy argued in 1938, "There can be no good thing in the CIO, for its ultimate [end] would be the destruction of the foundation of our present civilization and the substitution of a Godless, soulless State machine." John Frey, conservative president of the AFL's Metal Trades Department, argued that the CIO's tactics had the "hallmark of Moscow and [are] imported from Russia." There could be "no more compromise between Communism and American trade unionism," Frey claimed, "than there could be between Atheism and Christianity."[27]

These accusations received national attention in August 1938, when the newly formed House Committee on Un-American Activities investigated Communist infiltration in the CIO. In his 1938 HUAC testimony, Frey alleged that there were 280 Communists on the CIO's payroll and that party members had infiltrated both the Democratic Party and the Roosevelt administration. He characterized the favored and successful tactics of the CIO—sitdown strikes and mass picketing—as "frontline trenches in which the mass revolutionists of the future are to receive experience and training to equip them for the day when the signal for revolution is given."[28] While his charges of a Communist presence in the CIO often had more than a grain of truth, they had a limited effect within Detroit unions in the late 1930s as long as the alliance between Communists and the non-Communist left held.

This tenuous coalition shattered after the Molotov-Ribbentrop pact of August 1939 was signed. The Nazi-Soviet agreement caused party members, who before the pact had urged the United States to prepare for war against the Nazis, to oppose American interventionism. This flip-flop in the Communist Party's stand on the war shifted the domestic political terrain. A new right-wing anti-Communist caucus, led by Walter Reuther and including Socialists, Social Democrats, and members of the Association of Catholic Trade Unionists (ACTU), developed within the UAW.[29] The opponents of this Reuther group were part of an alliance of leftists and centrists who worked with and were often influenced by Communist Party members.

The Nazi-Soviet pact presented Reuther and the other members of the right-wing caucus with difficulties. Reuther, like Sidney Hillman of the CIO, believed that unions could best increase their power through a tripartite, corporatist policy in which the government acted as a powerful mediator/ arbitrator between management and labor. The beginning of the war offered labor a golden opportunity to implement this plan, since the primary role of the United States between 1939 and 1941 was to provide the Allies with industrial goods. Labor thus was thrust into a vital wartime position. However, a corporatist strategy required labor to surrender a certain amount of freedom and to silence some of its potentially subversive voices. Unions thus could not strike and shut down war production without appearing unpatriotic, so they would instead have to seek wage increases through the potentially weak mechanism of governmental bureaucracies.

The Nazi-Soviet pact threatened the creation of this tripartite system because Communists in the CIO vocally opposed the Roosevelt administration's support of the war effort. As a result, the anti-Communist faction in the UAW turned against Communists in the union. At the August 1940 UAW convention, Reuther's supporters backed a resolution that lumped together the dictatorships of the Axis powers and the Soviet Union and condemned the "wars of aggression of the totalitarian governments of Germany, Italy, Russia and Japan." In addition, the delegates passed a resolution that barred any member of an organization declared illegal by the United States government from holding union office.[30]

Two major strikes during the conversion period gave labor's opponents a perfect opportunity to attack unions. Allis-Chalmers and North American Aviation produced engines and airplanes for the military, and both corporations were known for their low pay and antilabor stands. The relatively new aviation industry would clearly play a vital role supplying the allies and defeating the Nazis. As a result, no matter how legitimate the workers' grievances were, a strike that halted military production made the union vulnerable to charges of disloyalty. This problem was exacerbated by the fact that Communist Party factions led both union locals. When the UAW local at North American Aviation struck in June 1941, UAW leaders rushed to the California plant to convince union members to end their walkout. The workers refused, much to the chagrin of union leaders. Many UAW opponents criticized labor's actions and claimed the strikes were part of the Communist effort to throw a wrench into the allied war machine. President Roosevelt, acting with the approval of labor's representative in the War

Production Board, sent in troops to break the strike and gave orders that the local leadership be arrested and fired. While Reuther did not support the use of troops, he recognized that such strikes threatened labor's place at the table. Reuther argued that the party was "making political capital of workers' legitimate demands . . . in order to sabotage defense production and to discredit the administration in Washington."[31]

The short-lived Nazi-Soviet pact proved to Reuther and his allies that the presence of Communists in CIO unions opened labor to charges of disloyalty and threatened labor's status in the New Deal state. Labor liberals like Walter Reuther believed that party members would favor the needs of the Soviet Union over the legitimate demands of American workers whenever these two came into conflict. In addition, they recognized that the new structure of labor-government cooperation required union leaders to maintain unity and quash disloyalty. Any union that had a vocal Communist leadership would find it difficult to keep such a unified presence.

Thus, on the eve of World War II, Detroit's population was booming, and its labor movement was growing rapidly. The newly created CIO received the support of workers in the city's massive auto plants, but the nascent movement found itself under attack because of the presence of Communist amongst its organizers. This became a much greater issue once the Soviets allied with the Nazis and the CPUSA changed its position on American entry into the war. Anti-Communist labor leaders turned against the party as Communist-led strikes made the union vulnerable to charges of disloyalty. The brief red scare of the conversion period ended once the Nazis invaded the Soviet Union and the Soviets became American allies. However, the issues that created the little red scares of the 1930s—labor influence and the centralizing power of the New Deal—would again roil the politics of Detroit once this alliance ended.

CHAPTER TWO

LABOR AND THE BIRTH OF THE
POSTWAR RED SCARE, 1945–1950

On October 7, 1945, *Detroit News* reader Dorothy A. Riis wrote a letter to the editor complaining about the "general strike trend in this nation." She argued that the 30 percent wage increase that the strikers wanted was part of a larger Communist campaign to convince the public to support "complete control by our Government over all private enterprise." The Communist Party, in conjunction with the "New Deal mob," had planned on "bring[ing] on these strikes as soon as the war ended to try to convince the unsuspecting American people that the Communistic way of having the Government control every word and action of the little man, would be more pleasing to us than our own individual freedom. We must not be convinced!" Riis agreed that "in union there is strength," but she warned that Detroiters should not be fooled by a "union run by foreigners who have no conception of what our America and our totally free way of life means to each and every one of us."[1]

Riis's letter appeared before any conservative movement existed in the United States. However, she, like many other Detroiters, began to articulate some of the central concepts of postwar conservatism—fear of big government, antipathy toward organized labor, and hostility toward communism that predated the Cold War. While the CIO had long claimed that the labor movement improved the standard of living and protected the rights of the average worker, labor's opponents rejected these assertions. They argued that labor threatened individual rights and endangered American liberties.

Conservatism grew from multiple roots. This chapter will explore one prominent source of this ideology. In it, we will see that a grassroots conservative ideology developed among a segment of Detroit's population during the years immediately after World War II in response to the power of labor and the legacy of the New Deal state. As scholars like Kim Phillips-Fein and Elizabeth Schermer have pointed out, postwar conservatism developed nationally in large part in response to labor's power. During the mid- to late 1950s, key business and political leaders like Lemuel Boulware of General Electric and Arizona Senator Barry Goldwater crafted a critique of the New Deal and postwar liberalism that placed the labor issue at the center of their ideology. Barry Goldwater, for example, moved the Republican party's focus away from "McCarthyite witch-hunts" and instead "helped introduce into mainstream political discourse the conservative argument that many routine, heretofore legal trade union activities were, in fact, corrupt, dangerous, and un-American because they impinged on American individualism." Delegitimizing labor and the role that labor played in the American political economy thus became a central issue in the development of conservatism during the late 1950s.[2]

This conservative ideology did not crystallize nationally until the late 1950s and 1960s. However, the same debate about the proper role of labor took place in Detroit during the 1940s and early 1950s. The fact that this conflict arose in the Arsenal of Democracy is not surprising, since Detroit was the most heavily unionized city in the nation by the mid-1950s. Despite labor's influence in Detroit, anti-CIO candidates won political office in some crucial local elections by linking labor to the Communist Party. But, as with Goldwater a decade later, the target of this anti-Communist language was not the Soviet Union or the CPUSA. Instead, it was the New Deal and organized labor.

World War II

Labor's size and strength grew rapidly in industrial cities during World War II. The federal government gave an enormous boost to wartime union membership when massive government munitions contracts made Detroit the Arsenal of Democracy. Under pressure from the National War Labor Board (NWLB), manufacturers provided unions with maintenance-of-membership agreements in exchange for unions' no-strike pledges. Any employee working under these wartime contracts had a limited period to withdraw from the union if they so chose. If they did not, workers had to remain union members in good standing. If they failed to pay dues, they would be both expelled from the union and fired. Thus, every worker hired by a manufacturer who had a maintenance-of-membership clause in his contract automatically became a union member. According to one labor historian, these clauses "proved to be the most crucial policy decision the government made to strengthen the power of unions."[3] UAW membership during the war thus grew rapidly and almost effortlessly to 1,065,000 in 1944.[4] By the end of the war, roughly 30 percent of the all American workers belonged to organized labor.[5]

Wartime contracts encouraged hundreds of thousands of black and white migrants to pour into the city to fill the jobs offered in Detroit's booming economy. In the process, these migrations remade the city. This influx was so large that one 1942 population survey found that of the 268 adults in the survey's representative sample, only 64 were natives of Detroit.[6] Almost overnight, the city's African American population doubled. At the same time, Detroit's unions grew to include almost half a million members.[7]

Not surprisingly, union growth and racial change quickly became the most divisive issues in Detroit's politics. A 1942 survey undertaken by the federal government sheds light on the tensions in this "boomtown." According to the study, a large majority of Detroit residents (61 percent) identified with workers rather than management. Yet, at the same time, a relatively large segment of the population (almost 40 percent) expressed antagonism toward unions and their New Deal allies. Detroit was obviously a community in which industrialization and unionization created a great deal of tension. Those respondents who identified with labor often praised unions for raising wages, protecting workers from arbitrary firings, and checking management's power to speed up production. As one interviewee stated, "It used to be a whole lot worse but it has improved since the union came in. . . . I remember one time coming out of the factory and not being able to stand. I had to sit down on the curb for awhile. My legs were like rubber, but they don't drive the men like that now."[8] Another long-time autoworker complained that, before the union, "Men who devoted the best part of their lives to working in a factory and then they would hire a new person, and then they would have to lay somebody off, it was just as likely to be the old worker as the new one who didn't know anything. Men who worked twenty or thirty years, deserved something better than that."[9] For these workers, the rise of the CIO and the New Deal laws that made union growth possible profoundly changed their lives. For them, both the CIO and the New Deal meant economic justice for those who had been most oppressed before union mobilization.

Such passionate, favorable opinions were matched by equally strong negative views. One Detroiter complained, "The union is reaching for all they can get while the getting is good. One of these days they are going to reach too far. All these strikes—the general public doesn't like it."[10] Another Detroiter protested, "The members are forced to join and that's not right. Nine out of ten don't want to, but they either do or lose their job. People shouldn't have to pay money for something they don't want to."[11] According to the 1942 survey, Detroiters who criticized unions "deplore open conflict with management, show a lack of confidence in union leaders, and evince some fear of unions behaving as a selfish political or economic pressure group in the community."[12] While prounion respondents perceived conflict as necessary to protect workers against arbitrary management, antilabor Detroiters viewed strikes as a sign that unions were selfish, radical, and overly political.

Not surprisingly, economic status shaped Detroiters' opinions of organized labor. As Tables 1 and 2 illustrate, executives, small businessmen, and white-collar workers expressed far more hostility toward unions than did factory and service workers.[13] Professionals and small businessmen also believed that unions were too strong. Some respondents associated this strength with the New Deal government. As one former salesman complained, "Nowadays you have to treat labor with kid gloves. You can't say, 'Do that or be fired' because of the union and because the Administration in Washington is behind the union." He argued that the situation could be improved with the "removal of government restrictions on management. The present Administration is strictly pro-labor and anti-business."[14]

As the statistics in this federal survey indicate, wartime Detroit was an economically and politically divided city. The majority of workers interviewed believed unions were either just about right in their strength or thought they were too weak. Conversely, executives, professionals, white-collar workers, and small businessmen were largely hostile toward unions, thought they

Table 1. Chief Antagonisms toward Economic Groups (%)

	Executives	Professionals	Small businessmen	White collar	Factory workers	Service workers
Groups toward which person is hostile						
Unions, strikers	25	23	33	44	18	15
Factory management	12	6	10	6	14	9
Rich, big business	0	12	13	3	7	5
New Dealers, Washington	13	12	10	12	4	5
Labor leaders	25	0	10	6	1	6
Frivolous workers	0	0	0	0	5	2
Radicals in unions	0	0	3	0	2	7
Organized labor	0	6	4	3	0	4
Women in the shop	0	6	3	9	5	7
Other	0	6	3	9	5	7
No discernible antagonism	50	53	43	38	55	51
Total (%)	125	108	129	121	113	111

(Note: totals exceed 100% because some persons expressed more than one antagonism.)

Source: "Table 24. Chief antagonisms toward economic groups," Rensis Likert Papers, Box 9, Office of War Information: Reports & Memoranda Folder, Bentley Historical Library, University of Michigan, Section III, 24.

Table 2. Are they (unions) too strong, too weak, or just about right
at the present time? (%)

	Executives	Professionals	Small businessmen	White collar	Factory workers	Service workers
Just about right	0	6	17	24	41	46
Too strong	25	47	47	35	21	18
Too weak	0	6	3	3	16	13
Don't know	63	6	17	12	4	5
Not ascertained	12	35	16	26	18	18

Source: Rensis Likert papers, Box 9, Office of War Information: Reports & Memoranda Folder, Bentley Historical Library, University of Michigan, Table 27. "Question: Are they (unions) too strong, too weak, or just about right at the present time?"

were too powerful, and believed that the government played a crucial role in maintaining union influence. Union strength, they claimed, jeopardized both American business and American liberty. As one small-business owner complained, unions "are too strong. If you don't belong to a union you can't get a job and it's not a free country any more when you have to do things you don't want to do."[15]

Many executives, small-business owners, and white-collar workers argued that unions threatened freedom and sought to expand their influence in government. When asked what he thought the union wanted to see come out of the war, one executive said, "Higher wages, closed shop, check-off, with the union having a unqualified voice on the councils of government and industry."[16] This expanding federal power and prolabor government seemed to some to endanger both democracy and capitalism. One interviewee even conspiratorially questioned, "Are we going to have any private enterprise after the war?" He claimed, "The average little man is beginning to feel the Government is getting too much control. Everything centers in Washington and pretty soon we are going to have to ask Washington if we can breathe."[17] Thus, according to this wartime federal survey, a prominent segment of Detroit's population objected to labor's growing power and associated it with an increasingly intrusive federal government. The New Deal labor laws that workers embraced appeared to many nonworkers to restrict business freedom and threaten democratic capitalism.

The 1945 Detroit Mayoral Election

The Detroit mayoral election held in the fall of 1945 marked the first opportunity for the city's residents to debate the issues that faced postwar Detroit. Given the enormous increase in labor's size and power, it is not surprising that the CIO became the focus on the election. However, the debate over labor's proper role occurred in the context of anti-Communism. The Cold War had not yet begun internationally, but Detroit voters responded to anti-Communist themes and reelected a previously unpopular incumbent because of anti-Communist sentiments. However, the source of anti-Communist rhetoric needs to be put in context; those beliefs had little to do with the Soviet Union or the Communist Party and a great deal to do with labor and race.[18]

In this first postwar local election, UAW leaders sought to take advantage of labor's wartime increase in size and power. They hoped to extend the CIO's influence into the political realm by electing one of their own as mayor. In preparation, the CIO Political Action Committee (CIO-PAC) added two hundred thousand new voters to the city's registration list in 1944. Organized labor, according to the *New York Times*, was making its "most ambitious bid to win control of a major city."[19] Richard Frankensteen, their chosen candidate, was a popular UAW leader with ties to the union's left wing. His opponent, incumbent Edward Jeffries, appeared vulnerable because his administration had done little to solve the key problems caused by the massive wartime population influx or the subsequent racial tensions.[20] A relatively quiet primary on August 7, 1945, gave little indication of the bitter final election to come. In this first round, Frankensteen won 44 percent of the vote while Jeffries received 37 percent. Under the nonpartisan system of Detroit elections, the two candidates with the most votes in the primary moved on to the general election in November. Frankensteen was clearly the favorite.

In order to overcome his deficit, Mayor Jeffries ruthlessly red baited his opponent during the general-election campaign. One pro-Jeffries pamphlet, for example, depicted a dripping red hand below a caption that read "Beware. The Issue: Labor's Control of City Government. The Opponent: Frankensteen. The Threat: Communism."[21] Jeffries thus painted his opponent as a puppet of organized labor, which he equated to the Communist Party. The mayor repeatedly claimed that he faced "ruthless and bitter opposition by a small group of men who want to get control of Detroit's Government so they can make a guinea pig of the City." These men, according to Jeffries "want the power that goes with control of Detroit's Municipal Government so they can make the City an experimental laboratory for their social, labor and industrial programs and ideas."[22] He depicted the national CIO Political Action Committee (CIO-PAC) as a shadowy cabal that sought to "reshape the government of Detroit and the nation to meet its own pet ideas of social and economic revolution."[23] Detroit, according to the mayor, was the radicals' first target because the city "is the industrial metropolis of the U.S. If the national PAC can succeed here, other communities must follow."[24]

The CIO-PAC, according to Jeffries, was an antidemocratic minority that sought to silence all opposition and extend labor's control into yet another branch of government.

A wave of strikes hit the city immediately after the war ended, which seemed to confirm Jeffries's warnings that the CIO sought greater power. This labor unrest changed the tenor of the election. Work stoppages became so common that the *Detroit News* ran a Strike Box Score, modeled after a baseball box score. In it, the paper listed which companies experienced strikes, how many employees were affected, when the strike began, and when or if it had ended. As the battle lines between CIO workers and management hardened, the antilabor local newspapers began a vicious campaign against the CIO and, by extension, Richard Frankensteen. The press seized upon the strikes as examples of labor's power and illegitimate interests. The *News*, for example, condemned an oil strike that had led to a shortage of gasoline throughout the city. The paper argued that the work stoppage was a form of coercion that was designed to force the government to intervene and settle the dispute in the strikers' favor. The *News* claimed that the strike "has the character of a general strike, in that its methods and aims are 'political'." Any political strike, according to the *News*, was an illegitimate extension of labor's power and scope.[25] The *News* thus objected, not only to the strike itself, but also to the political nature of the strike.

Letters to the editor supported the paper's antilabor diatribes and echoed many of the beliefs expressed in the 1942 survey. Bob Jones wrote to the *News* that he was just one of many area residents who was not only out of work due to union actions, but he was also out of gasoline because of the gas strike. Since the closest public transportation was more than two miles away, it was difficult to get food for his family. He sarcastically speculated that "maybe my wife and children will have to eat grass until these strikers get their selfish way."[26] "E. R." complained that "since the CIO and its goon squads took over the running of the affairs of the country we have had no such thing as a United States Government."[27] J. J. Appenzeller complained that he "can't see any democracy as long as any organization can dictate to the majority of the people what they can have."[28] Labor, these writers argued, threatened American democracy. Strikes privileged workers' demands over the larger public good. By asserting labor's rights over those of the majority, strikers threatened the majoritarian basis of democratic rule according to the *News* readers.[29]

Frankensteen struggled to overcome the perception that he represented only the CIO's interests by equating workers' needs with those of the public at large. "I don't know of a single thing that labor wants that every decent citizen does not want from his city—decent housing, decent transportation, and adequate recreation facilities," Frankensteen insisted. He repeatedly asserted that he would be a "Mayor of all the people," not just the spokesmen for radical labor.[30]

Frankensteen's strategy to equate labor's welfare with the public well-being was undercut when the AFL unions in the city decided to back Jeffries. Their critique focused on the potential implications for the AFL and the labor movement in general if the CIO candidate won. The AFL and CIO were engaged in a bitter conflict in Detroit, especially since the AFL perceived the CIO's growth as encroaching on its traditional territory. For example, at the end of the war, the UAW sought to insure employment for recently laid-off autoworkers by retraining them to do construction work on postwar public works. The Detroit Building Trades Unions, one of the largest and most powerful units within the AFL, bitterly attacked the CIO for pushing its way into these traditional AFL jobs. "Don't think for a minute," a delegate at a local AFL meeting shouted, "that the CIO will stop at the building trades. We should determine now to meet with full force the disruptive tactics of their goon squads."[31] As a result of this conflict, AFL leaders worried that Frankensteen's campaign was in fact part of a CIO attempt to "gain control of the City Hall in an effort to make it a citadel from which to crush AFL unions."[32] While the federation obviously had practical reasons for opposing the CIO's seeming power grab, it also had a more philosophical objection. "It was the abuse of power on the part of just such elements that accelerated the growth of totalitarianism movements in Italy and Germany," a *Detroit Labor News* editorial argued. "The present effort of the CIO to capture the city hall, if successful, will catapult the members of that organization into similar political efforts the country over. It will make out of a portion of the labor movement, a revolutionary political party which in turn will accelerate the demands for repressive legislation against all labor, and ultimately open class conflict, which unquestionably, this country cannot stand."[33] Thus, the CIO, if victorious, would continue its policy of "political" strikes, which, the federation feared, would lead to a backlash, complete with repressive labor legislation and the rise of a reactionary right wing. In portraying the CIO as a "revolutionary political power," the AFL sought to assert its volunteeristic views and restrict the CIO's more radical interpretation of the relationship between labor and government.[34]

As a result of the AFL's endorsement, Jeffries's backers could portray him as a candidate who opposed the "radical" and "selfish" CIO-PAC but supported the rights of labor and the public at large. Floyd McGriff, conservative editor of the *Redford Record*, insisted that the election was "not one of a labor mayor versus a business mayor," especially since the AFL, the "SECOND LARGEST LABOR BODY IN THE CITY" opposed Frankensteen [caps in original].[35] The Detroit Teamsters praised Jeffries as "a true friend of organized labor" who had abandoned the long-standing policy of using the police department as strike breakers and who had raised municipal employees' wages to the point that they were "as high or higher than that of any other large city."[36] As a result, Jeffries received the votes of many members of the white working class, who feared the "radical" policies of Frankensteen's leftist supporters. These workers could back Jeffries, who promised to protect the advances labor had made, even as he limited the left's power and "radical" agenda.[37]

Jeffries's campaign was ultimately successful: he won the final election 56 percent to 44 percent for Frankensteen. The incumbent gained 19 percent of the total vote between the primary and the final.[38] How influential were Jeffries's accusations? While Jeffries' charges might seem wildly exaggerated, and while the local press certainly fanned the anti-Communist, anti-CIO flames, the specter of CIO control over city hall energized voters. The 1945 election had one of the highest voter turnouts in the history of Detroit.[39] Clearly, fear of the CIO and all that it seemed to stand for brought many Detroiters to the polls. But who were these voters? According to two scholars of public opinion, Jeffries' received overwhelming support from native-born whites, particularly those of a higher socioeconomic status. A large majority of the residents in selected Polish, Italian, and Yugoslav neighborhoods—all heavily working-class ethnicities—supported Frankensteen over Jeffries.[40] There was thus a fairly pronounced class split in the voting. A majority of ethnic working-class Detroiters, many of whom were union members, supported Frankensteen. Nonunion, middle- and upper-class native-born whites overwhelmingly backed Jeffries. These were the same groups—executives, small-business owners, professionals, and white-collar workers—that expressed antagonism toward unions and New Dealers in the 1942 survey (see Tables 1 and 2). Many voters apparently agreed with Jeffries's portrayal of the CIO as a radical organization bent on social and political control. These same middle- and upper-class whites had told federal survey takers in 1942 that they feared unions behaving as a selfish political or economic pressure group. Thus, in one of the most heavily Democratic, prolabor cities in the country, a majority of voters supported a candidate who portrayed the CIO as a dangerous threat to American democracy. Just as Barry Goldwater would do fifteen years later on a national level, Mayor Jeffries successfully crafted an ideology locally that portrayed unions as treacherous, un-American institutions that threatened individual liberties.

Labor-Liberal Agenda

Frankensteen's 1945 defeat marked a setback for labor locally. However, union leaders continued their drive to expand labor's influence nationally. Although laborites disagreed among themselves on the critical question of Communist involvement in the labor movement, they agreed on crucial political issues. Even the traditionally conservative AFL by 1945 supported much of the labor-liberal agenda. The central aspect of labor's program was the Keynesian idea that high levels of government spending were necessary to maintain what the AFL and others called an "economy of plenty."[41] Liberals increasingly sought to create a high-wage, low-price economy that would avoid another depression by encouraging mass consumption and thus maintaining high levels of employment.[42] In order to avoid debilitating inflation, labor-liberals during the postwar period urged the federal government to extend price controls. Much of their agenda was incorporated into a handful of crucial pieces of federal legislation that was being debated in 1945 and 1946. The first was the Full Employment bill, which "recognize[d] that a right to useful work at decent pay should be the heritage of every American able and willing to work, and that the government has a duty to its citizens to carry out the obligation to provide jobs for all."[43] The second was the Wagner-Murray-Dingell social security bill (which called for "cradle-to-grave" social insurance plans). Liberals thus sought to expand the New Deal welfare state, and they spent much of the immediate postwar period fighting to further this agenda.[44] However, they quickly found that powerful business and political forces were arrayed against them. Conservative Republicans not only opposed this expansion, but they fought to roll back crucial New Deal legislation like the Wagner Act. As the election of 1946 (discussed below) illustrated, many voters turned against key elements of the labor-liberal agenda, especially price controls.

The 1946 Election

The 1946 election was fought over the issues labor liberals held most dear and conservatives opposed most adamantly. Both locally and nationally, opposition to union-backed price controls and criticism of CIO strikes were key components of the Republicans' strategy for winning Congress in the off-year election. Running on the campaign slogan "Had Enough?" the party benefited from the public's disgust with continued wartime price controls on meat and the Truman administration's inability to end the interminable postwar strike wave. By the fall of 1946, consumers across the country increasingly blamed the formerly popular Office of Price Administration (OPA) for severe shortages of meat and durable goods.[45] An October 1946 Gallup Poll found that 66 percent of respondents agreed that the next Congress should "pass new laws to control labor unions." A month later, Gallup found that 50 percent supported passing a law forbidding all strikes and lockouts for a year.[46] A poll taken shortly before the 1946 election by American Speaks found that the Republican Party gained 10 percentage points among Midwestern voters between the 1944 presidential election and the 1946 campaign. A pro-Republican editorial in the *Detroit News* credited the "interminable succession of strikes, for which the [Truman] Administration is blamed, both for inept handling of wage-price controls and by reason of its own political identification with the CIO wing of organized labor" for this increase in Republican support. In Detroit and in most other industrial cities, the *News* claimed, the "CIO-PAC and the Democratic organization are now virtually one, and equally the targets of the public's smoldering resentment of the strike record."[47]

The Democrats' inability to stop strikes and make goods readily available opened the way for Republican candidates to tarnish all Democrats with the brush of left-wing labor and "radical" governmental policies. Letters to the editor indicated that many voters equated both the OPA and the CIO to Communist bureaucracies. For example, Detroit resident William L. Moore wrote in a letter to the *Detroit News* editor that union support for the OPA was further proof about whom the CIO was really working for. "Doesn't Russia tell the people what they are to pay for all their commodities?" Moore asked. Such policies, counter to free enterprise as they were, indicated to this author that "the factions guiding the CIO are red and they hope to take the blue and the white out of the color of our flag."[48] Another letter writer complained to Walter Reuther that limited automobile production was "planned in Moscow. . . . The Communist OPA gang held everything down in order to help the CIO break the laboring man."[49] Thus, these writers equated price controls, formally a popular wartime liberal policy, with Communism. They also rejected a planned economy and the subsequent extension of government power inherent in the New Deal and the labor-liberal agenda.

In their critique of planning, some Michigan voters expressed their support for a libertarian ideology espoused by Freidrich von Hayek's *The Road to Serfdom*. Hayek's surprise 1944 bestseller was serialized in *Reader's Digest* in 1945, and its main argument was further popularized in a cartoon that appeared in *Life* magazine. *The Road to Serfdom* was an impassioned defense of free-market capitalism. Central economic planning, whether of the left or right, limited entrepreneurship and innovation, according to Hayek. Peacetime planning, he argued, led inevitably to disagreement as different interest groups rejected plans that hurt them. In the chaos and confusion that resulted, some people would turn to a strong man who could execute their plan. Thus, planning, according to Hayek, led inexorably to totalitarianism. The Austrian economist wrote this book because he had become progressively more disturbed by Western governments' increasing intervention in their nations' economies. Hayek advised his readers that such intervention threatened economic freedom, which Hayek argued was the precondition to all other freedoms. If the American government continued to regulate the economy as it had during the New Deal and war, Hayek warned, Americans would soon be living in a totalitarian state. Hayek's book quickly became a central work in the developing canon of conservative thought. Like Hayek, some Michigan voters argued that, no matter how well intentioned government intervention in the economy was, it would lead inevitably to a regimented economy and dictatorial, undemocratic state.[50]

Michigan Republican gubernatorial candidate Kim Sigler echoed this critique of planning during his 1946 run. In a Detroit radio address, Sigler claimed that the Michigan Democratic party "believes in the 'theory' of bureaucrats and regimenters in Washington."[51] Democratic candidate Murray Van Wagoner, the former state highway commissioner and governor, was not known as a New Dealer and had little support from the CIO or the state party. Sigler ignored these inconvenient facts and focused his criticism on the Michigan Democratic Party, which he claimed was "partly controlled by left wingers and communists."[52] He warned that a Democratic victory in 1946 would "give great impetus to the left wing movement in America" in the 1948 national election while giving "aid and comfort to the communist elements that are now using the opposition party as a vehicle with which to control this country."[53] After Van Wagoner complained that the Republicans were "crying communism for lack of a better issue," Sigler criticized the fact that his opponent "scoffs at warnings of communist infiltration into government. He can't see the things that may destroy America."[54] Instead, Sigler insisted, Communism was "quietly on the march in America." Democrats, he said, were tarnished with the brush of Communism because they had allied with and borrowed ideas from the Communist Party during the 1930s. Communists used this alliance to infiltrate American government and would continue to expand their influence as long as Democrats continued to give them "aid and comfort." Sigler's accusations tapped into voters' frustration with strikes, federal price controls, and food shortages, and he posited himself as the only candidate who could stop the seemingly relentless spread of left-wing ideologues into state government.

As in the 1945 Detroit mayoral election, Sigler's opposition to any extension of New Deal liberalism resonated with Michigan voters in the 1946 election. "Vote for Democrats? Phooey!" Florence Behenna of suburban Detroit wrote. If Democrats were elected, she claimed, returning veterans "won't have to pay high prices for food for there won't be any food. . . . They will have no shirts to wear, no meat to eat and no jobs. What a life! Give me the good old Republican administration any day."[55] A majority of Michigan voters agreed. Republicans won a resounding victory in the 1946 local and congressional elections and took control of both houses of congress for the first time since 1930. Sigler and the rest of the Republican ticket were swept to an overwhelming victory by a margin of almost three hundred thousand votes. Van Wagoner even failed to carry Wayne County, the traditional stronghold of the Michigan Democratic party.[56] The CIO-PAC was unable to mobilize a large labor vote in Wayne, despite Van Wagoner's warning that labor could either vote to consolidate the gains it had made under the New Deal or succumb to the "forces of reaction."[57] As one self-identified "CIO right winger" explained his support of Sigler, Stalin and the CP were "determined to keep their grip on this country that they made during the New Deal fiasco. . . . As all New Deal Democrats have this taint, let's make it a Republican landslide."[58]

"And so died the New Deal!" the *Detroit News* gloated after the election. "That strange political conglomeration is no more. For more than 13 years it has regimented and ruled and restricted the country, but now it passes."[59] In its post-election editorial, the *News* asserted that the New Deal's defeat meant that Communists and their liberal allies could no longer push their radical agenda of bureaucratic control through the federal government. Voters, the *News* claimed, had repudiated the New Deal's "leftist tendencies" and thrown their support behind a "competitive, free-enterprise economy."[60] Republicans and their supporters believed that the New Deal welfare state should not be expanded or continued but instead should be rolled back. Michigan voters rejected the liberalism of the war era, in which the government controlled prices and wages while supporting prolabor legislation. They agreed with the libertarian and anti-Communist themes articulated by Sigler.

The Michigan Red Scare

The crushing Democratic defeat in 1946 convinced many prominent labor-liberals that they needed to act decisively against Communists within the labor movement. In the increasingly hostile national and international environment, it was imperative that the CIO differentiate itself from the Communist Party in the public mind in order to protect the liberal agenda. Two weeks after the congressional election, the eighth annual CIO convention passed a policy statement that declared, "We . . . resent and reject efforts of the Communist party or other political parties and their adherents to interfere in the affairs of the CIO." Philip Murray, president of the CIO, argued that this statement "provides an answer to the slanders that have appeared in the public prints that the CIO is Communist-dominated."[61] Although the declaration didn't call for the CIO to take any action, it marked a change in the strategy of the CIO president.[62] Murray had long resisted calls to purge the Communists from the CIO, and he continued to reject such demands in 1946. However, the new political environment forced Murray to move away from his unity strategy and publicly distance the CIO from the Communists.[63]

Despite its shift to an anti-Communist policy, the CIO (and labor in general) quickly found itself under attack from the new Republican governor. The victorious Governor Sigler had vowed during his campaign to expose Communist infiltration, and he began to make good on his promise almost immediately after taking office. In the process, Sigler helped create a red scare in the state of Michigan. In February 1947, the governor ordered the Michigan civil service director to begin a loyalty investigation of all state workers and asked the state attorney general to scrutinize Foss Baker of the United Public Workers of America (UPWA-CIO).[64] This union had been created in 1946 from a merger of the left-led United Federal Workers of America and the State, County, and Municipal Workers of America. The UPWA was a heavily African American union that called for the then-radical demand that the government stop discriminating against black workers, who tended to work in the lowest-paying, most menial jobs despite their qualifications.[65] The UPWA also took the controversial stand that federal workers could strike and should be given the same rights that the Wagner Act provided nongovernmental workers. These positions grew out of the leftist politics of the UPWA's leadership, a number of whom were later identified as members of the Communist Party. Almost immediately after the UPWA was created, Congress and the U.S. Civil Service Commission criticized the union and warned that any federal workers who "actively supported" the Communist policies of the UPWA could be fired on the grounds of questionable loyalty to the nation.[66] Governor Sigler followed Congress's lead and accused Baker of organizing state workers "on the pretense of bringing them into a labor union when in fact he is interested in the Communist Party."[67] In response, the UPW removed Baker from his position. Sigler was praised by a number of Michigan citizens, one of whom wrote that the governor's action had "put Michigan in the vanguard of investigating subversive activities." Sigler's stand, according to the writer, would make him a "national hero [who] might become President of the United States in 1948."[68] Thus, Sigler successfully linked labor with Communism in the public mind. Even before President Truman created the Loyalty Security Board in March 22, 1947, to investigate federal employees, Governor Sigler successfully convinced many Michigan residents that Communist-led unions threatened the government. Sigler, like newly elected Republicans in Congress, was crafting a conservative ideology that combined libertarianism and anti-Communism. Much to the chagrin of labor liberals, this nascent ideology resonated with American voters in 1946.

Emboldened by his success, Sigler agreed to testify in front of the House Un-American Activities Committee. In his hyperbolic statement before HUAC on March 28, 1947, the governor asserted that there were fifteen thousand Communists and twenty-two Communist-front organizations in Michigan. He focused much of his attention on Communists in the UAW. Sigler stated that there was a "terrific struggle in the UAW-CIO in the city of Detroit by the Communists on the one hand, and the good loyal American citizens in that organization on the other, in an effort to gain control." He called the left-wing UAW leaders R. J. Thomas, George Addes, and Richard Leonard "captives of the Communist party," which he said meant that that they "follow the Communist party line in union activities." Sigler went on to claim that his administration had compiled the "necessary facts to establish conclusively that the Communists are striving to gain control of the labor movement in Michigan and in some instances have succeeded in the absolute control of certain unions."[69]

Sigler's assertions brought almost immediate condemnation from both the left and the right in the UAW. R. J. Thomas denied that he was a party "captive" and claimed that Sigler was "just saying these things because he's getting information from somebody inside our own organization."[70] Walter Reuther, who had up to this point been largely silent in response to Sigler's anti-Communist charges and who had not given much support to Sigler's opponent in the 1946 election, charged that reactionaries were "resorting to the traditional Red Scare" because they were "unwilling and unable to meet and solve the serious social and economic problems" which confronted the American people. Reuther went on to criticize Sigler's reactionary allies for launching a red hunt whose "ultimate victims are intended to be, not Communists, but all effective labor leaders and labor unions."[71] Sigler's attack had thus gone beyond exposing Communists and appeared to liberal anti-Communists to target labor as a whole.

This fear that the governor was going after unions was not misplaced. Shortly after Sigler appeared before HUAC, three important antilabor bills and one anti-Communist bill appeared on his desk. Of the three, one outlawed mass picketing, another gutted the Workmen's Compensation Act, and a third made strikes by state employees illegal. Lawyers employed by General Motors and backed by the major auto companies drafted much of this legislation.[72] The anti-Communist bill up for Sigler's approval was the Callahan Act, which required all members of foreign parties to register with the Michigan attorney general.

This legislation infuriated a number of prominent Michigan labor leaders from both the AFL and CIO, who recognized that these Republican proposals threatened labor's interests. The Michigan Federation of Labor passed resolutions urging the Governor to veto the labor bills.[73] Walter Reuther telegrammed Sigler to insist that these laws, if passed, would "greatly aggravate the causes of industrial unrest."[74] Gus Scholle, a prominent anti-Communist member of the UAW, complained that the Callahan act made it "possible to designate a union or other organization as a foreign agent" and thus could be used to destroy labor unions and other legitimate groups.[75] Despite CIO and AFL opposition, Sigler signed all four bills.

In response both to this threatening Republican legislation and to the success of conservatives, a group of labor-liberals crafted a long-range plan to seize control of the Michigan Democratic Party while simultaneously distancing themselves from the radical left. Labor-liberalism, they believed, could only be protected on the state level by making the Michigan Democratic Party into a mechanism that would perpetuate progressivism. Sigler's successful attack against Communists appeared to labor-liberals to create an environment in which antilabor legislation could be passed without significant public opposition. The Reutherites thus pushed their anti-Communist critique into the realm of local and state politics in order to protect union interests by differentiating themselves from popular-front leadership.[76]

The key figures in this process to seize control of the Michigan Democratic Party were Gus Scholle of the Michigan CIO; G. Mennen Williams, a Detroit lawyer who had served under former Democratic Governor Frank Murphy; and Hicks Griffiths, Williams's law partner. Despite Sigler's election-year rhetoric to the contrary, the Michigan Democratic Party had not been controlled by the CIO before 1947 and had not been much of a threat to spread the New Deal to state government. The CIO acquiesced to this arrangement until the Michigan Republicans threatened labor's interests in 1947.[77]

Scholle and the other labor-liberals had their first meeting on November 21, 1947. They drafted a plan for organizing Democratic clubs throughout Michigan in hopes of acquiring influence at party county and district conventions. A few months after this first meeting, the state CIO-PAC adopted a formal resolution stating that it intended to change the party into a "real liberal and progressive political party which can be subscribed to by members of the CIO and other liberals."[78] With both the CIO and the liberal Democratic clubs on board, labor liberals set out to accomplish two main goals: seize the machinery of the regular Democratic Party and elect G. Mennen Williams as governor.[79]

Surprisingly enough, given their fears of the CIO's power, the Detroit Federation of Labor threw its support behind Williams's candidacy. Clearly, they believed that Sigler's antilabor laws presented a far greater threat to the AFL than did the CIO. The political situation had developed much as the DFL leaders had feared: the presence of Communists in the CIO along with the CIO's repeated strikes had created an environment in which politicians could successfully pass antilabor legislation.[80] The AFL thus encouraged the CIO to purge itself of Communists while also working with it to push Sigler out of office.

At the same time Michigan labor-liberals were setting out to move the Democratic Party in a more progressive direction, they were also embarking upon a campaign to distance themselves from the Communists. This was part of a national movement to sever the connection between New Deal liberalism and the Communist Party, which culminated in the formation of the Americans for Democratic Action (ADA). Much of this battle between liberals and the radical left took place within the UAW and CIO. Walter Reuther, one of the ADA's founders, became the UAW president in March 1946 on an explicitly anti-Communist platform. His faction solidified control over the union by throwing their support behind the Truman administration in the burgeoning conflict between the United States and the Soviet Union and by criticizing the left-led UAW coalition for its continued support for the Popular Front.[81]

While anti-Communism was a core element of the newly developing conservative ideology, conservatives were not the only anti-Communists. Liberals began to move against their former Popular Front allies during the years after World War II. Some had been repulsed by Stalinist show trials and gulags during the 1930s, but they often continued to work with Communists as long as doing so did not harm their larger agenda. The Republican victory in 1946 indicated to many liberals that the time had come to end this alliance publicly. Walter Reuther, president of the UAW during the late 1940s, exemplified this move to the center. Reuther had grown up in a socialist household, and he had willingly worked with Communists to organize the UAW during the 1930s. However, the Communist-led strikes during the period from 1939 to 1941 confirmed to Reuther and his supporters that Communists had what he called "outside loyalties." He complained, "The Communists have a complete political valet service." However, their "customers" soon discovered that "they have become boxed in, thoroughly dependent, and pliable instruments of the party linemen."[82] Such "customers" thus quickly found that they could no longer oppose the party line, even if it conflicted with the best interests of labor. By 1947, Reuther recognized that labor-liberals were "living in a period in which there are going to be witch-hunts, hysteria and red-baiting by the most vicious group of congressmen that have gathered under the dome of the Capitol."[83] As the Truman administration created the loyalty-security board to fight Communists at home and adopted the Truman Doctrine and Marshall Plan to fight Communism abroad, Reuther argued that it would be political suicide for the labor movement not to clean house of anyone with outside loyalties. The passage of the Taft-Hartley Act in the spring of 1947 solidified Reuther's determination to move against Communists within the union. If UAW leaders refused to sign the anti-Communist affidavits the law demanded, the union could not participate in National Labor Relations Board (NLRB) elections and thus lost the protection of the federal government. As a result, delegates to the 1947 UAW convention supported Reuther's demand that union leaders sign the affidavits and defeated the remaining left-wing leaders within the union. In the long-running faction fight between the right-wing Reutherities and the left wing of the UAW, Reuther gave a crushing blow to his opponents. Shortly after the convention, Reuther also demanded that CIO unions not support Henry Wallace's Communist-supported candidacy for president. ADA liberals rejected a Popular Front strategy and turned against Communists in order to protect both their liberal agenda and the labor movement in an increasingly hostile, conservative political environment.

The 1948 Gubernatorial Campaign

The 1948 Michigan gubernatorial campaign was a battle between conservative Republicanism and resurgent New Deal liberalism. Governor Sigler once again red baited his Democratic opponent. The governor accurately

characterized G. Mennan Williams's campaign as part of the CIO's "ma-
neuvers to gain control of the state Government," which he called part of
a "pattern of political seizure that has brought ruin to many European
countries." Sigler continued to stress his anti-Communist credentials and
promised "continuous efforts to ferret out and curb subversive activities."[84]

However, Sigler's anti-Communist and anti-CIO campaign did not win
him the 1948 election. In his successful 1946 campaign, Sigler's platform
emphasized his opposition to price controls, strikes, and New Deal government expansion, as well as his anti-Communism. However, in 1948, Sigler
ran against the Communist Party and failed to articulate the libertarian
ideology that had been so popular in his previous campaign. The governor
so exaggerated the Communist threat in his campaign speeches that he
undermined his credibility. For example, one prominent state Democrat
attended a meeting in early 1948 at which Sigler was supposed to be the
principal speaker. According to the official, "Sigler was late. He finally rolls
up in a limousine with a motorcycle escort. He took the mike away from
the fellow then speaking and announced melodramatically that he had
been warned not to come. But he was there to defy the Communists." The
Democrat was so appalled by the governor's behavior that he told his wife,
"If after that kind of performance Sigler could win an election, I shouldn't
be in politics."[85] In a stunning upset, Democrat Mennen Williams defeated
Sigler, despite the fact that Republican Thomas Dewey carried Michigan
in the presidential election.

While politicians in other states successfully used red scares to solidify
Republican power, Michigan's 1946–48 scare had the opposite effect. Sigler's
loss indicated that many Michigan voters, despite their anti-Communist
rhetoric, were far less worried about Communists and far more concerned
with the labor-liberal agenda. As the 1945 mayoral and the 1946 gubernatorial elections indicated, some voters opposed elements of the wartime
New Deal. They embraced the libertarian critique of price controls and they
railed against the increasingly politicized and powerful labor unions. In both
Detroit and Michigan, postwar elections became referenda on the New Deal
and on the rights given to labor under the New Deal. In response to this
conservative threat, labor-liberals reinvigorated their movement. They articulated an ideology that incorporated Keynesianism and anti-Communism.
They abandoned more radical elements of the New Deal agenda, particularly
the demand for an expanded welfare state and full employment. By modify-
ing their agenda, Michigan labor liberals temporarily gained the upper hand
in their continuing ideological battle with conservatives.

The 1949 Red Scare in Detroit

As tensions between the United States and the Soviet Union increased in the wake of the Czech coup of 1948 and the Berlin blockade of 1948–49, fears of domestic Communist subversion intensified. In 1949, a red scare occurred in Detroit that focused on the city's municipal workers. The uproar began when a twenty-four-year-old city worker named George Shenkar passed his exam to become an assistant mechanical engineer for the Water Commission in December 1948. Because he had identified himself as a Communist, Shenkar was denied this promotion. Shenkar appealed the decision to the Civil Service Commission, which upheld the Water Commission's ruling. The issue then passed to the Detroit Common Council, which found that its hands were tied. Since the Communist Party was a legally recognized political party in the state of Michigan, and since the Detroit city charter forbade dismissal of employees for membership in any political party, the city had no legal means to fire Shenkar from his city job.[86]

Donald J. Sublette, the secretary of the Civil Service Commission, pushed the issue of subversion onto the front pages of the city's newspapers. He charged that Detroit had at least 150 Communists or Communist sympathizers on its payrolls, particularly in such key departments as the Water Board, Public Lighting Commission, and Health Department. Sublette argued that a handful of saboteurs could threaten the city's security: "For sabotage purposes, for disruption of production, for effective bacteriological warfare, and for many other things, local governments are far more important in the Communist takeover planning than the Federal Government," Sublette claimed. "The communists deliberately try to get into the essential service jobs where it would be easiest to produce chaos." Sublette particularly warned the public about the United Public Workers of America (UPWA-CIO), the largest municipal employees' union in Detroit with more than twenty locals in various city departments. Yale Stuart, a Russian-born labor organizer who lost an arm while fighting with the Lincoln Brigade during the Spanish Civil War, led the local branch of the UPWA.[87]

Subversion was not the only reason many Detroiters objected to the UPWA. Detroit voters' animosity toward municipal unions increased during the late 1940s as inflation pushed up both wages and taxes. The UPWA, a left-led and racially progressive union, successfully fought for higher wages during the inflationary postwar period.[88] But as city employees' salaries rose, Detroit property-tax payers became increasingly irate. When Mayor Jeffries proposed increased property taxes in 1947 to pay for the city budget, incensed homeowners who blamed him for giving in to the municipal unions berated him. "You have to crack down and get tough with those union heads or we will have no city government at all," wrote one constituent.[89] Another letter writer pled with the mayor to "reduce taxes and save Detroit and help save America." Lower taxes on homes, this unnamed homeowner argued, "means better security and drives out communism; high taxes and insecurity invites communism."[90] Clifford Knapp asserted that "our national security rests upon individual home security, and this must be inviolable."[91] Homeowners were becoming more and more frustrated as inflation increased the value of their homes and as property taxes soared. The inflationary spiral of the late 1940s seemed to trap these homeowners, and they focused much of their wrath on municipal unions. Like California homeowners in the late 1970s, these Detroit voters articulated a philosophy that equated high taxes with Communism and low taxes with homeownership, security, and Americanism.[92]

As a result of both fear of Communist subversion and long-simmering anger that many Detroit homeowners felt about high taxes, there was a great deal of public support for the drive to break the UPWA. Thus, when Sublette urged that all thirty thousand city employees be required to pass a loyalty check and take an oath that they were not Communist Party members, his proposal received widespread support. "If an [employee] refuses to take the non-Communist oath, he should be subjected to searching investigation," Sublette said. "If the investigation discloses he is a member of the [Communist Party] or an affiliate, he should be fired."[93] Police Commissioner Harry S. Toy seconded Sublette's proposal and stated that he could not see why "any citizen of the United States should object to taking such an oath." Mayor Van Antwerp, however, pointed out that the city had no legal right to do so.[94] As long as the state of Michigan recognized the Communist Party as a legal entity, he noted, the city could not fire an employee solely on the basis of political affiliation.[95] Nevertheless, the mayor appointed a three-man loyalty board—consisting of Police Commissioner Toy, Corporation Counsel Raymond J. Kelly, and Civil Service Commission President Chester A. Cahn—to investigate Communist infiltration among city employees and provide the mayor with a preliminary report no later than July 11, 1949.[96] Toy immediately ordered the police red squad to investigate city workers.[97]

The local newspapers played a key role in pushing the loyalty issue. All three dismissed the mayor's note of caution and called for immediate action. The *Detroit Free Press* demanded that George Shenkar be dismissed, while the *Detroit Times* sided with the police commissioner. The *Detroit News* recognized that Sublette's loyalty check most likely violated the city charter and so called for voters to pass a charter amendment to establish a city loyalty board and make membership in any subversive organization grounds for dismissal from any city job. In order to expedite the process, the *News* included a clip-and-send card addressed to Mayor Van Antwerp and members of the council that urged them to put the loyalty amendment on the ballot for the upcoming September primary.[98] City hall was almost immediately inundated with letters in favor of the loyalty amendment, most of which were on the *News*'s clip-and-send form. The following day, the mayor complied with the paper's proposal. "The moment I saw the front page editorial in the Detroit *News* today," said the Mayor, "I called [Corporation Counsel Raymond] Kelly and told him to prepare the amendments."[99]

Many Detroit residents responded eagerly to these anti-Communist measures. Jeffrey White, for example, wrote to Mayor Van Antwerp that his "drive against the Communists on the city payroll is one of the best things you have done for the city of Detroit."[100] Another supporter pointed out that the "typical communist procedure for gaining control of a nation" began with "comparatively mild labor legislation and a moderately graduated income tax." Eventually this led to the situation the nation now found itself in. "We now are afflicted with collective bargaining, unemployment insurance, an income tax, confiscatory in the higher brackets, increased privileges for labor unions, and economic nostrums and restrictions of all kinds, until employers have few rights except to meet the payroll, and the rest of us only the right to pay taxes." Unless the people woke up, this author warned, "the enslaving process will soon be complete."[101] Clearly, a number of Detroit residents perceived Communists in city government as an opening wedge in the left's seemingly relentless drive to push forward New Deal legislation. Interestingly, these critics focused on taxes and labor legislation rather than guns or bombs as the instruments that would ultimately destroy the United States. With the public seemingly behind the anti-Communist proposals, Detroit became the first city in the United States to create its own version of the Un-American Activities Committee.[102]

A mere four days after the Detroit Loyalty Committee was formed, it sent the requested July 11 preliminary report to the mayor. The committee generated a list of thirty-four city employees they believed should be investigated.[103] They reported that the police Subversive Squad had already begun to scrutinize these employees, but they did not feel that it was "wise to give names or present the evidence submitted until this investigation is completed." Thus, even before Detroit residents changed their city charter, the local Red Squad was already investigating the loyalty of suspected city workers.[104] In response to this report, the mayor asked Governor Williams to submit a proposal to the state legislature at its next special session that would deny the Communist Party the right to appear on ballots. This measure would then sidestep the city charter's prohibition against asking civil servants about their political party or affiliation: once the Communist Party was no longer legally recognized as a legitimate political party, the city would not violate its charter by asking an employee if he or she was a Communist.[105] The mayor's request to the governor received the backing of Community Home Owners Association of Detroit, which argued that "any organization advocating the overthrow of the existing government by means of force, instead of by democratic process of the ballot, has no valid claim on moral right to the protection of that government." Despite the fact that Communists at this point were guilty of nothing more than belonging to a legal party, Detroiters demanded that the city government remove them from their jobs.[106]

Local UPW leaders and their supporters reacted to the loyalty scare with anger. Yale Stuart, the Detroit UPW president, insisted that the Common Council was "attempting to divert public opinion from the fact that you are cutting the wages of the sanitation department [employees] . . . playing politics with the wage adjustments of thousands of the city's clerical, hospital, skilled and semiskilled [employees], [and] practicing unlawful discrimination against minority groups like the Negro and Jewish workers in city government." He insisted that the red-baiting campaign had nothing to do with increasing local security, but that it was instead a "camouflage for your political purposes in the midst of a campaign year."[107] The resolutely anti-Communist Detroit NAACP uncharacteristically agreed with Stuart and opposed the loyalty amendment because they feared that it would be "used as the Federal Loyalty probe was to unfairly charge and discriminate against Negroes and members of other minority groups."[108]

These complaints fell on deaf ears. The city council ignored Stuart's statement and subpoenaed him to force the UPW leader to answer whether he was a Communist. The *Detroit News* insisted that the union's opposition actually proved the necessity of the loyalty oath. "The louder the UPW cries out against the loyalty check" a *News* editorial contended, "the more sure may citizens be of the need." The *News* argued that Communist city workers did present a legitimate security threat, since they were "strategically placed for espionage—as is the case especially of any industrial city with a large role as a supplier of military equipment."[109]

As the pressure increased on the UPW leadership, local municipal-employee AFL affiliates distanced themselves from the UPW-CIO and used the loyalty issue as an opportunity to weaken their CIO rivals. Lawrence Piercey, international vice president of State, County and Municipal [Employees]

locals (AFL) commended city officials' efforts to rid the payrolls of subversive employees and demanded that the city refuse to recognize representatives of the "communist-dominated" UPW until they submitted non-
Communist affidavits, as his union had done.[110] Gordon Carnochan, the
president of Council 77 of the American Federation of State, County and
Municipal [Employees] (AFSC&ME-AFL) wrote to Mayor Van Antwerp
to inform him that members of his union did not "harbor any beliefs in
subversive methods or ideals which would now or in the future hinder the
service due the citizenry of Detroit" and "will gladly voluntarily sign an oath
of loyalty to our democratic form of government." Carnochan's union was
only too glad to push aside its left-led rival.[111]

UAW president Walter Reuther responded to the uproar in Detroit by
demanding that the CIO banish left-led unions like the UPW. "There is
a bloc of international unions controlled by the Communist Party in the
CIO," Reuther claimed. These were "paper unions, sitting on their charters,
using them for propaganda springboards and blocking the organizing of
millions of unorganized workers in these fields. The public workers have
30,000 workers organized out of six million in America," Reuther pointed
out. "What about the 5,970,000 who want a CIO union that is clean?"
On July 12, 1949, the UAW-CIO convention adopted a nearly unanimous
resolution demanding the expulsion of eleven unions, including the UPW,
from the national CIO.[112] In early November 1949, the CIO did just that.[113]
In response to conservative fears of subversion and high property taxes,
liberals moved against a Communist-led municipal workers union in order
to protect the labor movement against accusations that it was affiliated with
Communists. Conservatives had long railed against taxes and unions, to little
effect. However, in the superheated atmosphere of the early Cold War, the
conservative argument that union power and high taxes could undermine
the nation resonated with Detroiters.

The Korean War and the Garbage Workers' Strike

Union power, high taxes, and anti-Communism continued to roil Detroit
politics between the summer of 1950 and the summer of 1952. During
these years, the local red scare reached its peak as a result of the Korean
War. The 1949 loyalty amendment was implemented for the first and only
time during this period. Throughout the summer of 1950, the front pages
of the local newspapers kept up a steady drumbeat of bad military news
from Korea while debating how Detroit should prepare for a seemingly
inevitable nuclear attack. In this fearful atmosphere, Detroit residents will-

ingly supported both state and local attempts to check subversion and root out Communists from their midst.

Once again, the focal point was the United Public Workers. Late in August 1950, Mayor Cobo responded negatively to local municipal workers' demands for a raise. Two days later, sanitation workers who belonged to the now-independent UPW picketed city hall for two hours to request an immediate pay hike. According to the new UPW leader Louis Segadelli, the workers planned to march peacefully and then return to work. However, Mayor Cobo, who had been tipped off that the UPW was about to engage in a work stoppage, invoked the 1947 Hutchinson Act against the workers and fired them. This state law, which made it illegal for any public workers to strike, had never been implemented. Under the act, any employees who "knowingly" violated its provisions could lose their jobs. Fired workers could reapply, but they forfeited all seniority and pension rights and had to start at the bottom of the seniority ladder.

After firing the UPW workers, Cobo then set out to break the strike and discredit the leftist UPW leadership. He held out an olive branch to workers who wanted to return and vowed to punish the strike leaders. Cobo informed the sanitation workers that if they had not realized that they were breaking the law by striking, they could file a petition within ten days in order to regain their jobs, along with their seniority and pension rights. "I feel that not all of the sanitation division [employes] who failed to work Thursday knew they were violating the law," Cobo stated. However, Cobo and Carl Warner, the public works commissioner, affirmed that they would never rehire any worker who had "knowingly" disobeyed the Hutchinson Act. "We'll put the fear of God into them forever," Warner threatened.

CIO and AFL leaders supported the mayor and urged their members to cross picket lines. They pointed to the UPW Communist leadership to justify their stand. Alex Barbour, secretary-treasurer of the Wayne County CIO, argued, "In this particular strike we believe [Cobo] should distinguish between the leadership and the rank and file." The UPW leaders, Barbour reasoned, were "not above exploiting the rank and file. Fifteen years' experience in the labor movement has taught me that some of their leaders could be accused of Communist affiliations."[114] Edward Frey, president of the Detroit Municipal [Employees] Association, hinted darkly, "We are inclined to believe the demonstration was not totally inspired because of the wage situation—that a far more sinister motive may be involved."[115] Local labor leaders thus distinguished between a legitimate union demand and a politically motivated and potentially subversive act in order to check the growing popularity of the conservative criticism of labor.

Less than a week after Cobo fired the picketing employees, local UPW leaders called off the strike and capitulated to Cobo. The mayor informed the garbage workers that there would be no pay raise, but that they could be considered for reinstatement with seniority if they filled out an application. Ultimately, all but seven workers who submitted the required papers were rehired.

Cobo's actions won him overwhelming praise. Letters to the mayor's office, which reportedly favored Cobo by 50 to 1, indicating the growing popularity of the conservative criticism of unions.[116] A letter to the *Detroit News* editor complained, "Ever since communism and unionism have gained such a stranglehold on America there have been few public officials who seemed to have much respect for the sacredness of the laws of this State or Nation." Mayor Cobo, this author wrote, deserved great praise, since "under the present administration union leaders are not running this City. That is as it should be."[117] Dorothy Trumble wrote the *News* that "the unions have become so powerful that they can upset our whole economy. Instead of demanding higher wages, which in turn bring on higher prices, they could work together and bring down unreasonable prices and return us to a normal prosperity."[118] As they had since the New Deal, a segment of Detroit's population complained that unions retained too much power and that they acted in their own selfish interests, even if their demands led to crushing taxes and higher prices. They equated labor with Communism and argued that both threatened the nation.

Labor and Modern Conservatism

No organized national conservative movement existed in the late 1940s. However, a conservative ideology was developing in places like Detroit during this period. These conservatives articulated an antitax, libertarian philosophy that developed in response to the New Deal state, particularly the state's support of labor. Conservatives complained that unions had too much power and used it in ways that were often detrimental to the public good, as when they demanded higher wages. Conservatives also embraced anti-Communism, even before the Soviet Union presented a strategic threat to the United States. In the two crucial elections that occurred shortly after the war—the 1945 mayoral election and the 1946 gubernatorial race, conservatives equated Communism with organized labor and its attempts both to extend its power and spread its pro-welfare-state message.

This was a powerful and popular agenda during the period immediately after World War II. Politicians and, as we'll see later, businessmen certainly fanned the flames of this antistatist ideology. However, these ideas clearly resonated with many Detroit residents, especially the small businessmen, executives, and white-collar workers who complained to a wartime federal survey that unions acted as selfish political or economic pressure groups. When Governor Sigler shifted his focus away from labor and the New Deal and toward the Communist Party in his 1948 reelection campaign, he lost. The heightened Cold War tensions of first 1949 and then the Korean War shifted the political focus, and much of the anti-Communist discourse centered on the Soviet threat abroad and the threat of Communist subversion at home. However, labor and the expanding welfare state would become a crucial issue again, after the Korean War came to a stalemate and Cold War tensions cooled during the late 1950s.

CHAPTER THREE

RACE AND ANTI-COMMUNISM, 1945–1952

In February 1952, Coleman Young, the executive secretary of the left-led National Negro Labor Council (NNLC), defiantly testified before the House Committee on Un-American Activities (HUAC) when it came to Detroit to investigate Communism in defense industries. While many witnesses shrank before HUAC's harsh light, Young attacked the committee for targeting local black leaders and for being led by a segregationist. He castigated HUAC Chairman John Wood, who was from Georgia, for his bigoted pronunciation of the word "Negro" and forced Wood to apologize. He denounced segregation and pointed out that "in Georgia, Negro people are prevented from voting by virtue of terror, intimidation, and lynchings. It is my contention you would not be in Congress today if it were not for the legal restrictions on voting on the part of my people." When asked if he would serve in the armed forces if the Soviets were to attack the United States, Young asserted that he had "fought in the last war and I would unhesitatingly take up arms against anybody that attacks this country. In the same manner I am now in the process of fighting discrimination against my people. I am fighting against un-American activities such as lynchings and denial of the vote. I am dedicated to that fight and I don't think I have to apologize or explain it to anybody."[1]

Young's defiant statement made him a hero for many in the Detroit black community. "I felt like Joe Louis home from a title fight," Young later said. "People called out my name as I walked down the street, and small crowds gathered when I stopped." Someone even made a phonographic record of his testimony, which circulated in African American neighborhoods for all to hear. But the hearings had a very different effect in other parts of the city. Disturbing racial incidents occurred in some Detroit factories after an FBI informer provided HUAC with the names of black and white workers who were current or former Communists. One African American employee in a Chrysler plant, for instance, was threatened by his fellow laborers and hung in effigy. At Midland Steel, a crowd of white workers taunted a black laborer with such threats as "Let's throw that red in the barrel" and "Let's lynch the Nigger." At the American Metal plant, a dozen men threatened John Chervney, a white man, with a rope. One member of the group yelled, "I am from Georgia, [Congressmen] Woods' state. I'll show you how we do it there."[2]

Black liberals, on the other hand, were largely silent on the subject of HUAC's hearings. The *Michigan Chronicle*, the local black-owned newspaper, gave only a brief mention of the fact that the committee had subpoenaed prominent black radicals. The paper didn't reprint Coleman Young's fiery denunciation of HUAC's racism. Nor did it discuss any of the disturbing racial incidents that occurred in Detroit factories.[3]

These three very different responses to Young's testimony—that of African Americans on the street, white vigilantes, and black liberals—reveal much about the complex relationship between race and anti-Communism and the development of liberalism and conservatism during the early Cold War. The enthusiastic response Young received as he walked through black neighborhoods in Detroit illustrated the appeal that left-led organizations held for many African Americans. Like Young, the Communist Party had long defied segregation. The white workers who attacked the Communists at the Chrysler and Midland plants used traditional racial epithets and scare tactics like lynching and hanging in effigy. While the targets of all of this vigilante justice were Communists, the rhetoric used against them did not emphasize the Communists' disloyalty to the nation. Instead these workers equated Communism with civil rights. As the threat against John Chervney showed, the vigilantes were determined to reassert racial hierarchy and punish anyone who undermined segregation. Although their violent response was extreme, the vigilantes' desire to maintain segregation was not unusual. In fact, 68 percent of respondents in a 1952 survey of whites in Detroit proposed that the city deal with its racial problems through some form of segregation.[4] The black liberals who ran the Detroit NAACP and printed the *Michigan Chronicle* fought to desegregate the city. However, they sought to distinguish their fight from that of the Communist Party. The liberals' silence speaks volumes about how they perceived the Communists. They did not celebrate the Communists for either their defiance or their martyrdom, thus refusing to equate liberals' struggle against segregation with that of the party.

Conservatism in Detroit grew from multiple roots. This chapter will explore the second prominent source of this ideology—the debate over race. As is true with the argument over labor and the welfare state, the question

of race was central to both postwar liberalism and to the rise of conservatism. Much of the political discourse that occurred in Detroit and Michigan
politics during the early Cold War was in fact a debate over the proper role
of government on the issue of race rights. In this debate, we can see the
limits of New Deal liberalism. On one side, liberals and their leftist allies
supported the New Deal's pledge to create a nation of homeowners, and
they hoped to extend that promise to both blacks and whites. They also
backed wartime fair-employment policies, and they sought to continue these
job protections into the postwar era. In response, conservatives promoted a
far more limited government role, and they often equated racial liberalism
with Socialism and Communism. They argued for the right to segregate
neighborhoods and workplaces, and they deeply resented liberal and leftist
attempts to desegregate Detroit.[5]

Wartime Racial Conflict

Race became a crucial issue in Detroit during and after World War II.
Between 1940 and 1950, Detroit's African American population doubled
from 149,000 to 300,000 as black workers streamed into the city to fill
the good jobs that Detroit's booming manufacturing sector offered. Yet, as
in other northern cities, black migrants experienced problems. They found
that their housing options were confined to a relatively small segment of
the central city. Most blacks in Detroit lived in segregated, over-crowded
slums, particularly in a three-and-one-half square-mile area sarcastically
named Paradise Valley. Likewise, many migrants found that certain jobs
were typically reserved for whites, leaving the worst types of employment
to African Americans.

The influx of African Americans triggered a large racist reaction. In a
wartime survey of Detroiters, more than one-third of the respondents expressed outright antagonism toward black migrants while an additional
third supported housing segregation.[6] These sentiments existed across class
lines in the white community (see Table 3). Fifty percent of small businessmen expressed hostility toward African Americans, while between 35 and 38
percent of factory workers, executives, and professionals were antagonistic.
"They are overflowing Detroit," one small businessman complained. "I
certainly wouldn't want to live next to one myself."[7] This businessman, like
many other interviewees in this poll, insisted that he was not racist. "We are
all American citizens," he said, "but I do think they are allowed too much
freedom." In particular, this man, like many other white Detroiters, wanted
restrictions on where African Americans could reside. As another respondent

stated, "They ought to settle them in one place like they have done with the Jews in Poland. They should have a section set aside for them and be kept there."[8] Respondents complained that property values declined when African Americans moved into white neighborhoods; they supported segregation as a way to maintain their communities while providing African Americans with a place to live. White Detroiters thus embraced restrictive covenants, homeowner improvement associations, and federal and municipal housing policies that kept the growing black population geographically hemmed in.[9]

In response to the discrimination African American migrants faced, Detroit's civil rights organizations boomed. Communist-led groups like the National Negro Congress (NNC) and the Civil Rights Congress (CRC) were two of the most active civil-rights organizations in the city during and immediately after the war. The Communist Party had long made a concerted effort to organize African Americans, whom they saw as the most subjugated and exploited segment of the American proletariat. During the early 1930s, the party achieved a major propaganda victory amongst African Americans when it successfully prevented the execution of the Scottsboro boys. The party had a well-deserved reputation for its battles against Jim Crow. Because Communists were so active in the fight against segregation, many whites associated civil rights with Communism and dismissed civil-rights demands as Communist agitation.[10]

Table 3. "How do you feel about the way Negroes fit into the community here in Detroit?" (%)

	Executives	Professionals	Small businessmen	White collar	Factory workers	Service workers
Shows sympathy or acceptance	25	24	27	15	6	13
Shows no antagonism but desires segregation	25	35	13	38	29	29
Shows antagonism	37	35	50	32	38	33
Shows fear of Negroes	0	0	3	0	7	9
Seems indifferent	0	0	3	9	3	0
Is a Negro	0	0	0	3	11	14
Not ascertained	0	6	4	3	6	2

Source: "Table 34," United States Department of Agriculture, "Detroit People in Perspective: A Survey of Group Attitudes and Aspirations," Rensis Likert papers, Box 9, Folder 9–41, Office of War Information: Reports & Memoranda Folder, Bentley Historical Library, University of Michigan. Note that in the original, the Executives column did not add up to 100 percent; it has been reproduced herewith as it was originally published.

The most prominent civil rights organization in the city, the Detroit branch of the NAACP, grew to more than twenty-five thousand members during World War II to become the largest NAACP chapter in the nation.[11] Created in 1909 to fight racial prejudice, the NAACP was a reformist organization that had the reputation during the 1910s and 1920s for expressing the interests of the black elite and middle class. During the Great Depression, the NAACP shifted its focus. It began reaching out to black workers and forming alliances with labor unions, particularly the nascent CIO.[12] In Detroit, the UAW and the NAACP worked closely in the drive to organize Ford, the largest black employer in the area. While the NAACP allied with Communist-led organizations during the war, it sought to distinguish civil rights from Communism.

As African Americans and local civil rights groups increasingly asserted themselves in wartime Detroit, conflicts over housing, jobs, and equal access to public space exploded. One of the largest controversies developed in 1941, after Detroit officials announced that they were going to build public housing for African Americans to help alleviate the city's housing shortage. The Sojourner Truth housing project was to be located outside of the narrowly defined black neighborhoods of Detroit. In response, white homeowners in the area created the Seven Mile–Fenelon Improvement Association to protest the project. They were particularly upset that the Federal Housing Authority refused to insure any more mortgage loans in the area because of the planned black public housing.[13] Caving to neighborhood pressure, government officials flip-flopped and designated Sojourner Truth as a white housing project. However, a coalition of liberal and leftist civil rights groups successfully rallied to convince the government to keep its commitment to make the project available for black families. After months of petitions and protests, a pitched battle between black supporters and white opponents broke out as the first African American families moved in. In the subsequent riot, almost forty people were injured and more than two hundred arrested.[14]

The decision to allow African Americans to move into Sojourner Truth infuriated members of the neighborhood improvement association. They were particularly incensed at the activities of Communist Party members and their allies, especially R. J. Thomas, the president of the UAW. In a series of letters written to protest black occupancy of the housing project, a number of writers stated that they were members of the UAW but rejected the stand taken by President Thomas. They complained of the "Reds in the CIO like Thomas who haven't got anything to do with the taxpayers of Detroit" and insisted that Thomas did not speak for them.[15] Rudolph Tenerowicz, congressman from the district that included the housing project, claimed that the party was behind the fight to insure that Sojourner Truth would be set aside for African Americans. This, he claimed, was merely a "continuation of the Communist program of using the Negro race as a spearhead of a false conception of race equality."[16] The Communists behind this campaign "live many miles from the locality of the housing project and have no intentions or desires to move into the immediate vicinity." The congressman's assessment that Communists played a crucial role in the fight for Sojourner Truth was correct. Tenerowicz was not red baiting his opponents as a means of discrediting them. Communists and their allies, such as Rev. Charles Hill, really were at the forefront of the Sojourner Truth campaign. Congressmen Tenerowicz raised a number of themes that became common among opponents of desegregation. Communist outsiders who were merely using the issue of racial equality to push a radical political agenda, these adversaries claimed, led the civil rights fight. Nowhere in this rhetoric was there any sense that civil rights advocates had legitimate complaints. Instead, this language depicted community members and taxpayers as the victims of a radical racial agenda.

Housing was not the only racially divisive issue in wartime Detroit. Conflict also developed in the workplace as whites in a number of auto plants, including Packard and Hudson Motor, walked off their jobs and refused to work with African Americans. Before World War II, blacks in the auto industry had been largely confined to the worst or the most unskilled jobs, generally in the foundry or in janitorial work. However, during the war, labor shortages, governmental persuasion, and union activism allowed black workers to move into jobs traditionally held by whites. The UAW and NAACP systematically pressured the federal government to uphold wartime Fair Employment Practices (FEP), thus forcing corporations to make more jobs available to black workers. While enforcement was irregular, the Fair Employment Practices Commission opened well-paid, semi-skilled work to blacks, often to the consternation of white workers.[17]

As in housing, Communists played a prominent role in the fight for fair employment. At the UAW annual convention in 1943, delegates from Local 600, a left-led organization with a large African American membership, called on the UAW to create a fair-practices department in the union. A department focused on fighting discrimination, they argued, would receive more resources from the union than would a mere committee. In addition, the FEP department chair, who the delegates assumed would be an African American, would integrate the currently all-white UAW executive board. Communists and their progressive allies in the UAW, including George Addes, Richard

Frankensteen, and Nat Ganley, supported the resolution, while members of Walter Reuther's faction opposed it on the grounds that it constituted reverse segregation. After a year of argument, the UAW established its Fair Practices Committee, which had fewer institutional resources than a department. The executive board retained the right to appoint the committee chair, thus keeping the board white and preserving the tenuous balance between left and right that existed on the UAW executive board. While the UAW's Fair Practices Committee was not as powerful as the leftists had hoped, it still played a crucial role in pressuring the federal government to abide by wartime fair-practices orders. In addition, George Crockett, the first chair of the committee, quickly built close ties to Detroit civil rights organizations and prominent Detroit radicals.[18] As in the Sojourner Truth housing battle, the effect of this activism was to help convince many white workers that radicals were behind the drive to pressure manufacturers to conform to fair hiring practices.

In response to these attempts to desegregate neighborhoods and ensure fair employment practices, a number of white Detroiters protested about their loss of privilege and speculated that New Dealers and radicals were behind these changes. "They are trying to equalize them and it will never work," one man grumbled to a wartime interviewer. "The politicians depend upon the Negro vote," another Detroiter complained. "Washington is backing them up to the limit."[19] One worker asserted, "Somebody is feeding them a lot of baloney about the white people suppressing them. I don't think it's as bad as they make out." He protested that black migrants were "crowding us out too much" and predicted, "There's going to be a race riot here one of these days."[20] All of these respondents viewed racial inequality and segregation as perfectly acceptable. Only the machinations of outsiders, who were supposedly using African Americans for their own political goals, were leading blacks to protest against their status and demand equality. Many whites, as the last interviewee stated, viewed themselves as the victims who were being crowded out of their jobs and neighborhoods.

Not surprisingly, racial conflict exploded in 1943. Wartime surveys clearly showed intense white opposition to the growing black population and equally acute frustration on the part of blacks. The race riot began at Belle Isle, as more than one hundred thousand blacks and whites packed into this popular public park on a hot summer day. Interracial fights broke out and quickly spread to the rest of the city as rumors of a race war swept through both black and white communities. During the conflict, black residents of Paradise Valley looted white-owned stores, and a crowd of almost ten thousand whites rampaged through black neighborhoods. By the end of the riot, thirty-four people had been killed, twenty-five of whom were blacks; 675 people had suffered serious injuries; and 1,893 people had been arrested.[21]

A liberal coalition dedicated to solving racial conflict began to coalesce in Detroit in response to the 1943 riot. Race became a crucial issue during World War II for liberals, who argued that the hatreds expressed in the riots contradicted the nation's democratic and equalitarian ideals. The war marked the beginning of civil rights as a component of the liberal agenda. While Communists had long made racial equality a central component of their ideology, white liberals had not. During the 1930s, the Roosevelt administration avoided racial issues as much as it possibly could. Despite the persistent efforts of organizations like the NAACP to convince FDR to back civil rights legislation, Roosevelt refused to do anything that would alienate the southern Democrats who controlled key congressional committees. He recognized that his support for any legislation that challenged the southern system of white supremacy could endanger his recovery agenda in Congress. World War II forced the administration to confront race. The wartime migration of almost two million African Americans from the rural South to the urban North increased black voting power and made African Americans a significant force in the Democratic Party. A. Phillip Randolph's threat to lead a March on Washington in 1940 pushed Roosevelt into Executive Order 8802, which promised fair employment on all government-funded projects during the war. The Double V campaign—Victory Abroad against the Axis and Victory at Home against Segregation—proved a popular civil-rights campaign. The administration, like many liberals, recognized that the United States could hardly support a fight abroad against enemies whose ideologies were based on racial superiority while still maintaining a system of racial hierarchy at home. The war, as Alan Brinkley has pointed out, "changed America's racial geography economically, spatially, and ideologically."[22] Thus, in the mid-1940s, racial liberalism became part of the larger liberal agenda.

The war as well as the wartime riots brought together groups of African Americans, Jewish and Catholic activists, and intellectuals who linked the battle against racism with the need to extend the American creed to African Americans.[23] The coalitions that formed as a result of this perceived need were heavily influenced by social scientists, particularly from the intercultural education movement. The members of this movement, the most famous of whom was Gunnar Myrdal, sought to bring reformers and experts together to use social science research to create policy and achieve social change. Supporters of the intercultural education movement believed that state-led social engineering, controlled by social science experts, could solve racial problems.[24]

Detroit social scientists weighed in with their opinions on riot prevention and racial amelioration almost immediately after the 1943 uprising. Alfred McClung Lee and Norman Humphrey, sociologists at Wayne University in Detroit, suggested that the city form a committee to gather data on racial conditions in the community. This board would channel intelligence to a central office that would formulate actions to reduce racial tensions. Humphrey and Lee's suggestion became the basis for the Detroit Interracial Committee, which was led by a trained social-service executive named George Schermer. Under Schermer, the Interracial Committee became an umbrella group at the center of a liberal interracial coalition that included the Detroit branch of the NAACP, the Michigan Committee for Civil Rights, the Urban League, the Citizen's Housing and Planning Council, the Detroit Council of Churches, the UAW Fair Practices Committee, the Jewish Community Council, and the *Michigan Chronicle*. Although these groups often disagreed on particular issues, they shared a strategy to depoliticize key municipal racial issues by solving them through a public-private partnership between experts, members of the city government, local civil rights groups, and local businessmen. This coalition became the key liberal force in Detroit race relations and sought to establish itself as a viable alternative to the Communists.[25] Their experiences in World War II encouraged liberal leaders to think that American capitalism could be a tool to improve blacks' economic, political, and social status. They, like liberals throughout the United States, justified their support for civil rights by referencing the American creed, the belief that the United States was based on ideals of liberty and equality. They hoped that this would be a powerful weapon to use to convince white America of the justness of their civil-rights cause. The liberal strategy was on display as the liberal coalition confronted the three largest issues black Detroiters faced during the postwar period— housing, police brutality, and job discrimination. In the clashes that occurred over these three issues, conservatives bitterly opposed liberal attempts to end segregation, and they continued to equate civil rights with Communism. In response, liberals distanced themselves from the Communist Party and sought to decouple civil rights from Communism. While liberals achieved little success during the late 1940s and 1950s, their battles to dismantle segregation in Detroit helped create a grassroots conservative ideology.

Housing and Race

The 1945 municipal election marked the beginning of a protracted debate over the nature of postwar society and the role of government. In addition to the question of labor's power (discussed in chapter 1), race and housing policy were prominent issues in the election. When mayoral candidate Richard Frankensteen was asked about his "position on bi-racial housing and on the preservation of neighborhood racial characteristics," he answered that he believed that "the main problem is inadequacy. We need modern housing for everyone in Detroit, and in the Negro sections particularly."[26] This position led Mayor Jeffries to portray Frankensteen as a supporter of African Americans while Jeffries depicted himself as the protector of white neighborhoods. In a speech on the northwest side, Mayor Jefferies reportedly asked his listeners whether they "want a Sojourner Truth housing project in this neighborhood."[27] His campaign played on racial fears by having campaign workers phone white homeowners to tell them, "The property owners of Detroit are anxious to re-elect our Mayor." After reminding listeners that they didn't "want the C.I.O., which is communistic, to control the City Hall," they then brought up what they called the "racial issue." Heavily black wards voted overwhelmingly for Frankensteen in the primary, campaign workers pointed out. "Frankensteen must have promised them something!"[28]

According to the community papers published by conservative Floyd McGriff, the "something" that Frankensteen and Common Council candidates like Rev. Charles A. Hill promised to the African American community was mixed-race housing. McGriff, the Hearst-trained editor of a chain of popular Detroit community newspapers, claimed that the "racial issue—suggesting, promoting and urging the location of negroes in white neighborhoods" was an issue "chiefly because Communist fronters, such as Rev. Charles A. Hill, negro candidate for [Common] council, and his playmates, want it pressed."[29] In the *Home Gazette*, McGriff printed a picture of Adam Clayton Powell addressing a Frankensteen rally and stated in the accompanying article "Powell has been a Communist front man for many years, agitating the colored people along Communist lines. He was brought to Detroit chiefly to assist Frankensteen and Hill."[30] McGriff repeatedly reiterated the connection between civil rights and Communism.

McGriff and other opponents of mixed race housing emphasized the idea that government action to help African Americans move into white neighborhoods would hurt white workers by lowering their property values. These property holders had been inspired by the New Deal's promise to create a nation of independent homeowners, and they eagerly responded to Roosevelt's assertion of the right to a decent home in his "Second Bill of Rights." Thousands of Detroit workers took advantage of the subsidized home loans and guaranteed mortgages offered by the Federal Housing Authority (FHA) and the Home Owners Loan Corporation (HOLC). But, because the HOLC and FHA would only guarantee mortgages in racially homogenous neighborhoods, these homeowners (correctly) perceived that mixed housing threatened their property values.[31] In a special Polish-language edition of the *Home Gazette*, McGriff contended that Detroit's Poles opposed any attempts to change their home neighborhoods since "most Polish home owners are factory workers who spent many years paying off their homes with factory wages." "It is no light matter," McGriff pointed out, "to a working man to see his home values shrink when negroes move into his area. There have been cases where a home costing seven thousand dollars was finally sold for one-fifth of its original investment when negroes moved into the neighborhood."[32] McGriff depicted civil rights as a zero-sum game; African American gains in housing could only come at the expense of white homeowners.

Mayor Jeffries was ultimately reelected with tremendous support in native-born white wards composed largely of small homes. As Floyd McGriff interpreted the election results, homeowners in "restricted white areas, determined that their home investments, representing in most cases a lifetime's work, were not to be jeopardized and reduced greatly in value by negro infiltration, voted their sentiments." White Detroit homeowners opposed Frankensteen because they "[did] not appreciate the negroes being whipped up into 'take over now' creeds, as suggested by Communist Policy and negroes in places of leadership."[33] McGriff discredited attempts to portray equal housing as merely an extension of the rights embodied in the New Deal. He helped craft a successful conservative critique of civil rights in which he combined anti-Communism with an argument that any government attempt to desegregate a neighborhood would deprive white homeowners of their property by lowering their home values.[34]

Liberal civil-rights leaders interpreted the 1945 election differently than McGriff had. The campaign made it clear to them that the fight for race rights would be hampered as long as their opponents could successfully dismiss their demands as communistic. African American liberals like Gloster Current of the NAACP argued that the city's failure to solve the housing problem created a situation that was "certainly ripe for the infiltration of Communists . . . and if a considerable influx does occur, it may be expected that confusion and strife will result." Since Communist organizations often sought to publicize issues through mass action, any Communist attempt to solve the housing issue would potentially inflame racial conflict and further embolden white opposition groups. Current proposed that liberals could "insure the community against a large scale infiltration" by "removing grounds for unrest in the Negro community."[35] Current's proposal encapsulated the strategy liberals followed during the late 1940s—grapple with the crucial problems the African American community faced while distancing civil rights groups from Communists and opposing any mass action that might inflame white opposition.

Current's proposal raises an important question: Why did black liberals oppose Communism, even though Communists were often the most vocal supporters of the fight to improve African Americans' status? Activists and leftist historians have long condemned black anti-Communists for their complicity in the American government's campaign to squash the radical left and their embrace of a conservative, court-based civil-rights strategy. As Manning Marable has written, "The failure and tragedy of [the NAACP's] conservative approach to social change was in its parochial vision and tacit acceptance of the Cold War politics." By refusing to work with the Communists, who were often the most committed antiracists, Marable argues, black middle-class organizations set back the fight against segregation and failed to take advantage of the window of opportunity that opened to African Americans immediately after World War II.[36] Recently, scholars like Eric Arnesen and Manfred Berg have criticized historians who have viewed the Party and its civil rights activities uncritically. According to Arnesen, these scholars have largely ignored both the "voices of contemporary African American opponents of the party" and the "willingness of [the Communists] to sacrifice black interests on command from the Comintern."[37] My analysis builds upon Arnesen's argument. Detroit liberals complained that the party was largely interested in "furthering the policies of the Soviet Union." The party, they claimed, supported civil rights only to the extent that this would help the USSR. Liberals fought to distinguish themselves from the Communists and insisted that race rights were central to the American democratic ethos.[38]

In the years after World War II, black liberals and leftists largely agreed on goals—expanding African Americans' access to housing, ending job discrimination, and stopping police brutality. However, they fundamentally differed on strategy. Liberal tactics were shaped by their fears that Detroit was a racial tinderbox. Liberals knew that much of the black community felt frustrated by the slow pace of change in the key issues that confronted the black community. However, they also recognized that many white Detroiters felt threatened by the social upheavals the city was experiencing, that these white voters controlled the city's government, and that some whites occasionally used violence to silence black demands.

Early in 1946, Gloster Current warned the city that the severe housing shortage and the Detroit Housing Commission's policy of segregation were leading directly to a "rapid rise of racial tension and conflict in Detroit." Current was both a key member of the liberal coalition in Detroit and an outspoken anti-Communist. In 1941, Current became the Detroit NAACP's full-time executive secretary. During the war, he worked closely with local black trade-union leaders to battle job bias in Detroit's factories and played a crucial role in helping to strengthen the ties between the local NAACP and the UAW.[39] After the war, Current was instrumental in the Detroit NAACP's campaign to open private housing by dismantling restrictive covenants. In 1946, Current sent the city prosecutor a list of ten violent incidents that occurred when blacks attempted to move into white neighborhoods, and he cautioned the prosecutor that "local 'hate' groups are stirring up trouble which, if unchecked, will soon cause another riot." Even though most of these incidents happened when black families bought private housing, Current blamed Detroit's segregated public housing policy for the violence. The city's support of segregation, according to Current, "has crystallized the attitude in Detroit that white people have a moral and just right to prevent Negroes from moving into so-called white neighborhoods where they perforce may choose to live."[40] Current, like other liberals, portrayed civil rights as a moral issue. The United States, civil rights activists argued, failed to live up to its democratic creed.

White homeowners relied on restrictive covenants to preserve the racial homogeneity of their neighborhoods. Current argued that these were the "most pernicious and undemocratic legal document[s] which Negroes are presently facing in the fight for adequate housing." He complained that "because of the unholy alliance between the courts, the improvement associations, the Housing Commissions and Federal authorities throughout the area, . . . the Negro is continually being hemmed into smaller and smaller living space with continued evils of overcrowding."[41] Because federal home loan policies favored racially stable, homogeneous communities, real estate developers and brokers encouraged neighborhood improvement associations to enforce restrictive covenants by suing either black residents of white neighborhoods or any neighbor who sold to blacks. Improvement associations in turn urged white homeowners to band together to stop the "influx of colored people."[42]

Current fought to end restrictive covenants through the courts, and he rejected the Communists' criticism of the NAACP's legal strategy. "Maybe the NAACP program is not spectacular enough to capture the imagination of the masses of working Negroes, but certainly it is basic for their welfare," Current argued. He criticized the Communists for "chang[ing] their line too often," and he characterized those African Americans who did support the Communists as "either dopes or opportunists."[43]

Rather than adopting mass action, as the Communists advocated, Current and the Detroit NAACP fought against segregated housing by challenging the legality of restrictive covenants. They hoped that working through the courts might allow them to negate the political power of the vocal white homeowners' groups. The Detroit NAACP's case, *McGhee vs. Sipes*, began when Minnie and Orsel McGhee moved into a white neighborhood on the northwest side. The Northwest Civic Association brought suit against the McGhees on the grounds that the entire neighborhood was covered by a covenant that prevented any house from being sold to or occupied by anyone "other than one of the Caucasian race." The Northwest Civic Association won in both the Wayne County Circuit Court and the Michigan Supreme Court, but McGhee and the NAACP prevailed in the U.S. Supreme Court in 1948, when the Court ruled that it was a violation of the 14th amendment for state courts to enforce restrictive covenants.[44]

The NAACP's victory created jubilation among many black liberals. The *Michigan Chronicle*'s editor believed the decision "opened the gate on greener pastures for the generations which will succeed us. More than this, the foundation has been laid for the building of a new era of inter-racial goodwill and true American unity." While liberals praised the ruling for allowing blacks to live anywhere they wanted, they also believed the Court had reinforced their belief in the power of the American system to end racial discrimination. One black Detroit resident who had been forced out of his home due to a restrictive covenant stated, "After I got over the emotional shock, I reflected on the meaning of the decision and felt that this is another reason for having confidence in Democracy." The NAACP's 1948 victory appeared to confirm the liberals' belief that they could use the tools of American democracy to integrate African Americans into mainstream American society. The Supreme Court had agreed with the NAACP's contention that the Constitution provided legal justification to the civil-rights battle and to the attempt to dismantle segregation. In the ongoing battle between liberals and conservatives, the Court's ruling against restrictive covenants struck a blow for liberals' belief that the American creed would successfully justify their battle to end segregation.[45]

Conservatives disagreed, and they organized in response to their defeat. The Small Property Owners of Detroit, a citywide organization of independent homeowners that was "brought into existence to defend our life-savings," stated that they would do everything in their power to elect city officials who would protect their property from the "threat" of integration.[46] Rather than seeing the Supreme Court's decision as a moral victory against antidemocratic forces, conservatives argued that integrated housing threatened property rights and hurt their economic status.

Detroit conservatives found their spokesman in the 1949 mayoral election. They threw their wholehearted support behind Albert Cobo, a bland bureaucrat with strong ties to local bankers and builders. His opponent was Common Council president George Edwards, a prominent anti-Communist progressive and labor activist. The local CIO leadership assumed that the popular Edwards would win handily in such a union stronghold, especially since he had distanced himself from the radical left and thus shielded himself from the accusations of Communism that had badly damaged Richard Frankensteen in the 1945 mayoral election.[47] Liberals failed to understand the depth of anger that white homeowners felt toward any organization that supported open housing and thus threatened the value of their homes.

The key issue in the 1949 campaign once again was housing. Edwards agreed with the liberal strategy of using government—whether through the courts or through local or federal policies—to desegregate. Edwards had long supported African-American attempts to buy homes outside of the narrow confines of the Paradise Valley ghetto. He also backed efforts to build public housing in outlying neighborhoods, away from traditionally black areas. Albert Cobo, on the other hand, opposed this policy and instead argued that new public projects should be located in slum clearance areas. Cobo objected to federal efforts to desegregate the city and instead insisted, "The values of single homes should be maintained. They cannot be when government housing projects area built in areas where single homes predominate—in the outlying sections."[48] By emphasizing "government housing projects," Cobo portrayed government, not as a force for equality, but as an entity that could threaten the property rights of white homeowners. Cobo's demand for a smaller government, of course, ignored the role that federal housing policies played in creating those areas of single-family homes that Cobo and his supporters so fiercely protected. But his stand was in keeping with the demand of groups like the Small Property Owners that government should serve those who pay taxes rather than those who consume them. Edwards quickly found himself under attack from white homeowners, many of whom were union members. On Detroit's east side, for instance, one UAW organizer reported that many members refused to put Edwards' posters in their windows because they disagreed with his housing program stance.[49]

Some neighborhood improvement organizations equated Edwards with the NAACP and its "radical" policies, an especially damning charge in the wake of *McGhee v. Sipes*.[50] Other improvement associations argued that Edwards's stand on public housing would undermine homeowners' rights.

White Detroit homeowners and their allies in the real-estate business worried about the implications of the new federal Taft-Ellender-Wagner housing bill, which promised to fund the building of five hundred thousand new public housing units in the next ten years. Members of the improvement associations feared that Edwards was likely to side with civil rights groups and support black public housing in white neighborhoods when the city received the newly acquired federal housing funds. The Detroit Real Estate Board, which supported the neighborhood improvement associations, reminded voters that "a welfare-state mayor and council" would support policies that were "just another way of killing the freedoms of man and putting business into the hands of socialistically inclined bureaucrats."[51] Edwards, these groups claimed, endangered white homeowners through his support of expanding the New Deal vision of affordable housing to African Americans. The associations insisted that they were not "preaching racial intolerance" since they believed that the "colored race are as human as we are and should be given every chance to work and enjoy life among themselves." Instead, these homeowners insisted, they merely wanted to maintain a "clear cut boundry [sic] between the residences of the two races."[52] The homeowners associations and the real estate board couched their opposition to Edwards and his housing policies in the language of limited government rather than racism. However, they sought to limit government only when welfare-state policies threatened white homeowners and undermined segregation.

Not surprisingly, black residents of previously white neighborhoods found themselves under attack as improvement associations fought to keep neighborhoods white. The Mayor's Interracial Committee received reports of "a cross-burning in another neighborhood, heated threats of violence at meetings in three different areas of town." Unoccupied homes that were under construction on the northeast side and were intended for black occupancy were set on fire. Local neighborhood groups were dismissing the drive for desegregated housing as "Communist or Socialist inspired," according to George Schermer of the Interracial Committee. "[T]he old stereotype of the Communist, foreigner, Jew or Negro, and the Communist tactic of exploiting the symbol of the minority group martyr, all these together," Schermer argued, "have the potential for creating a wave of anti-minority group, anti–civil rights sentiment which may reach extreme proportions." While white homeowners used the language of anti-Communism, their real opponent was not the Communist Party. Instead, they equated Communism with civil rights and the expanded welfare state, especially when such a government was used to desegregate. They used the rhetoric of anti-Communism to mask their racism, possibly even to themselves.[53]

George Edwards and his labor-liberal supporters were slow to recognize that white working-class homeowners perceived desegregation policies as a threat to their property rights. Edwards's campaign attempted to appeal to working class voters by portraying Cobo as the business candidate. He repeatedly castigated Cobo for his ties to special-interest groups, like the Board of Commerce, reactionary Detroit daily newspaper publishers, bankers, and big real estate tycoons who resided in posh Detroit suburbs like Grosse Point and Bloomfield Hills. He argued that these groups supported Cobo because they wanted to shift taxes from "industrialists and downtown stores to home owners." Edwards thus tried to portray himself as the defender of working class rights against the encroachments of big business. Liberals failed to recognize the growing appeal of small government, anti–welfare-state rhetoric amongst white Detroiters of all classes.[54]

Edwards's campaign convinced few white homeowners, who found Cobo's opposition to public housing very attractive. In response to a city plan to build thirty-two thousand public housing units, Cobo argued that such facilities should only be provided when absolutely necessary. The plan proposed that nearly 10 percent of Detroit's families would be given access to new public homes, a figure that Cobo believed was far too high. Instead, Cobo asserted, the city should buy large plots of land in the "blighted central districts," clear the slums, replat and rezone, and then sell the land to private real estate interests.[55] Cobo's appeal swayed white homeowners. The Small Property Owners of Detroit, for instance, extoled that, with Cobo, they at last had "a man we can support with pleasure, without mental reservations." Even heavily blue-collar areas like Detroit's west side backed Cobo over the UAW's candidate. On November 8, 1949, Cobo defeated Edwards by more than 105,000 votes out of almost 530,000 votes cast.

Edwards's mayoral defeat was a harbinger of the challenges liberals would face nationally during the 1960s, 1970s, and 1980s on racial questions. Decades before presidential candidate George Wallace appealed to suburban Detroit voters with his racist, antigovernment platform, conservative homeowners in Detroit embraced the critique of civil rights articulated by conservatives like publisher Floyd McGriff. Rather than viewing civil rights as an extension of constitutional liberties, as liberals did, conservatives saw it as a campaign that threatened white homeowners' property rights. Small government, in this context, meant protecting white neighborhoods from desegregation and using tax dollars to benefit tax payers rather than the poor. Conservatives crafted a small-government philosophy that portrayed big government housing policies as a threat to their freedoms and their property rights. They viewed themselves as the taxpayers who were being forced to pay for someone else's housing, even as their home values were threatened. Homeowners associations created a grassroots mobilization that fought against any attempt to desegregate white neighborhoods, and they elected a mayor who would speak for their interests for much of the 1950s.

Many Detroit whites responded to the perceived racial threat by leaving the city in the years after the war, eagerly taking advantage of federally guaranteed home loans and mortgage interest deductions to buy new suburban homes, despite the contradiction between their actions and the small-government rhetoric many espoused. Between 1950 and 1960, the white population of Detroit fell by 23 percent as whites moved to the suburbs. They brought with them their conservative philosophy, hardened in the racial crucible of Detroit, and established white suburbs largely protected from the "dangers" of desegregation.

Police Brutality and the Leon Moseley Case

Housing was not the only issue that liberals and conservatives, blacks and whites battled over during the post–World War II era. Police brutality, a longstanding problem for African Americans in Detroit, became another one of the key subjects the liberal coalition sought to solve in order to remove grounds for unrest in the African American community. Conservatives, however, discounted African American complaints as Communist propaganda. Yet another in a long line of brutality cases began on June 4, 1948, when Officer Louis Melasi shot Leon Mosley, a black teenager, in the back as the youth attempted to flee from a car he had stolen. Eyewitness accounts indicated that Melasi and his partner John Boland had badly beaten Mosley, so he should have been easy to subdue without resorting to gunfire.

This shooting happened against a long-term backdrop of tensions between police and the black community. George Schermer of the Detroit Interracial Committee regularly sent private letters to Police Commissioner Harry Toy asking him to meet with civil rights officials to iron out potential problems before relations between the police and black community worsened. Mosley's killing brought the simmering tensions to a boil. Edward Swan, executive secretary of the NAACP's Detroit branch, warned city officials that he had been receiving constant phone calls from all sections of the black community demanding that the NAACP take action in response to Mosley's killing. The NAACP had eyewitness statements that led Swan to believe that the shooting was either murder or manslaughter.[56] In response, George Schermer sent a letter to Police Commissioner Toy and Mayor Van Antwerp in which he implored them, "Something needs to be done immediately to calm the people and to convince them that the Police Department will do the right thing." Schermer claimed that witness reports were widely credited, leading the "average citizen to believe that firearms were resorted to after the boy had been in custody, and in spite of the fact that the boy could have been brought under control by the officers present." He warned, "[T]he city faces, right now, because of this incident, the greatest threat of interracial bad feeling we have experienced since the end of the war." He claimed, however, that an incident could be avoided if the police commissioner took positive steps, including suspending the officer who shot Mosley and meeting with a group of community leaders to assure them that no judicial whitewash would occur.[57]

The Communist-led Civil Rights Congress quickly organized community protests after Moseley's death. They demanded that the police officers be prosecuted, the Moseley family compensated for their son's shooting, and that Police Commissioner Toy be removed from office. The CRC stated their demands at a large demonstration at Mosley's funeral and at a march on city hall that attracted thousands of participants. The NAACP and other liberals were worried that Communists in the CRC were increasing the party's popularity in the black community with their high-profile protests against the Mosley killing. They also feared that this would link the Mosley protests with Communism in the minds of many white Detroiters. To avoid these problems, Schermer urged the commissioner to "Avoid all mention of activity by Communist groups. We know they are active and are exploiting this thing to the limit. However, because feeling is so general and because responsible civil and church leaders are taking the major leadership in expressing concern over this incident, any comment about Communists in this matter will be mis-interpreted." He further emphasizezd, "Our feeling is that the ground must be cut away from the Communists by taking positive action on the issue along the lines we have suggested."[58]

Liberal civil-rights leaders, worried that they were losing control of the situation, entered into a coalition with the CRC in hopes directing the alliance and moving it away from the Communists' strategy of mass protest. By allying with the CRC, the NAACP and its liberal allies hoped to express their outrage at the killing, ensure that the Communists could not use the issue to increase their standing in the black community, and squash any unrest that might arise out of a mass-action campaign. The liberals met with Police Commissioner Toy, much to the anger of the CRC, and asked that the officers be temporarily suspended until the public storm blew over. In response to such pressures, law enforcement officials agreed to an inquest into Moseley's death, and the police department suspended officers Melasi and Boland until the investigation was completed.[59]

The liberals' strategy of quashing mass action was on public display at Mosley's funeral on June 11. A few hours before the service was to start, Oscar Cohen of the Jewish Community Council warned Police Commissioner Toy that the Communists might use the funeral to provoke a riot. He worried that "if the situation [a riot] does not arise spontaneously—which it might because of feeling in that neighborhood—the Communists will attempt to provoke the police into a fight. We are afraid of a considerable disturbance." While the Communists distributed inflammatory leaflets, promising, "We shall fight that the murder of this child shall be avenged," the NAACP and its allies used the city's assurance of an impartial inquest to calm the crowd of mourners. The Rev. H. H. Coleman of the Greater Macedonia National Baptist Church advised the funeral congregation, "No public demonstration aimed at whipping up racial feelings to a white heat can solve the problem. Let our legal processes have a chance. Be calm. We have laws." George Edwards, Detroit City Council President and prominent ally of the UAW, encouraged the driver of a labor organization's sound car to leave the funeral and not use his public-address system to whip up the crowd. These peacekeeping efforts worked. The crowd, both outside of the funeral service and in the subsequent protest march to City Hall, remained peaceful.[60]

Yet not every city official distinguished between the Communists and the civil rights liberals, and some members of the city government attempted to delegitimize the protest by arguing that every activist pushing the Moseley issue was a Communist. This claim led to a series of scathing editorials in the *Michigan Chronicle*, the city's African American paper. According to the *Chronicle*, "It is not enough to say that the demonstration last week was led and instigated by communists and that therefore it did not mean that Negroes and liberals of the city are most vehemently protesting against this shooting." In fact, the *Chronicle* argued, such willful ignorance on the part of city officials strengthened domestic Communism: "Every city official who sat back in his office last week and said to himself that 'this is being pushed by the communists, we don't need to worry,' should put himself at the head of the long list of people who are not doing their share to make democracy work and are guilty of aiding and abetting the communists." By ignoring the legitimate complaints of the outraged black community, city officials had created a vacuum that the CRC was only too willing to fill. Reverend Horace White, a prominent anti-Communist and prolabor minister, complained in his weekly *Chronicle* column that the Communist

Party and its allies in the CRC were not actually interested in Moseley death "except that it served as a basis for getting the ear of many non-suspecting people of the Negro community, who wanted something done about a nasty killing in the city." White, like Gloster Current before him, saw the Communists as opportunists who merely used racial conflict in order to further the party's interests.[61]

The city's agreement to conduct an impartial inquest appeared to strengthen the liberals' shaky leadership. The situation seemed to calm down in the wake of this agreement, especially when the Detroit daily newspapers printed details of Mosley's killing that supported black complaints of police brutality.[62] However, this peace quickly ended once again after the judge handed down his verdict in Melasi's case in December. Judge Arthur E. Gordon rejected the findings of the coroner's jury and exonerated the patrolman who shot Mosley because he claimed that the eyewitness accounts had been gathered and manipulated by Communists in the NAACP. Judge Gordon wrote, "One group [of witnesses], which had been herded into the office of Ernest Goodman, the brains of Maurice Sugar's law office in the Barlum Tower, by some of the pink members of the NAACP, insisted dramatically that from two to seven police officers beat the driver with pistols and fists, until he escaped from them and that Patrolman Melasi shot him in the back while he was running or staggering away." Gordon complained that "the witnesses who made the wildest accusations of the beating . . . were of the group produced by the NAACP and sent to the Barlum Tower to be interviewed by the pink devotees of the agitation." The judge thus delegitimized the NAACP's complaints of police brutality by implying that Communists and their supporters fabricated the charges. The NAACP, according to the judge, was "pink"—not quite red, but still devoted to unjustified agitation.[63]

Judge Gordon's verdict made the NAACP and its allies in the Interracial Committee furious. Schermer sent Gordon a scathing letter in which he all but called him a fool. He pointed out that Mr. Goodman, who Judge Gordon had characterized as a "pink" agent of the NAACP, was not a member of that organization but was instead acting in the name of the CRC, a "known Communist front organization." Schermer leapt to the NAACP's defense by pointing out that "while a protest group organized by the Civil Rights Congress were whipping up support for a march on City Hall, the NAACP was cooperating with a number of other organizations to prevent a demonstration getting out of hand, was making factual representations to the press, was pleading with the Mosley parents to place their interests in the hands of persons or an organization that would seek redress through legal and orderly channels." He further noted, "It was not just the Communists or the NAACP that demonstrated horror and protest over the shooting of Mosley." Instead, Schermer pointed out, "The entire Negro community and much of the white community *believed* it was unjustified. Ministers, school-teachers, labor and civic leaders and many substantial citizens wanted the facts to be sifted out in court. They were not being 'pink' in insisting upon legal action." He scathingly accused Judge Gordon's comments of serving "the forces of hate and subversion well. Nothing could be better designed to build a sense of distrust in and anger at the forces of the law."[64]

The Mosley case pointed out once again the equation some Detroit whites like Judge Gordon made between Communism and civil rights. White opponents during the 1940s and 1950s could safely dismiss African American accusations of police brutality as Communist agitation rather than legitimate protest. Few white Detroiters supported African Americans in their persistent complaints against police brutality. Instead, they continued to back the police department and Commissioner Harry "Shoot First" Toy.[65] Although the term "tough on crime" appeared later, most white Detroiters likely would have agreed with the premise during the late 1940s and early 1950s.

In the 1940s and 1950s, crime and the need to crack down on criminals was not yet a key issue for conservatives. It became one during the early 1960s. By that time, Detroit's white population had fallen by 360,000 while the black population grew by 180,000. Many whites felt under threat by the burgeoning black community and its demands for equality. One response to this seeming peril came from the city's newspapers, which increased their reporting on crime and race. The *Detroit News*, for example, wrote that "blacks constituted 26 percent of the city's population, [but] they were responsible for almost 65 percent of serious crime." The Detroit police continued to engage in brutality, and civil rights groups continued to organize in response. They achieved little success until 1961, when a coalition of civil rights groups helped defeat Louis Miriani, the mayoral incumbent. Miriani, who succeeded Cobo as mayor in 1957, supported a crackdown on crime that led to widespread police harassment and intimidation against African Americans. The police campaign began after two white women were murdered in the winter of 1960–61. The *Detroit Free Press* and the *Detroit News* covered the crimes heavily and emphasized the race of the likely murderers. As crime hysteria gripped the city, Herbert Hart, the Detroit Police Commissioner, developed a plan that called for increased police patrols in high crime neighborhoods. Mayor Miriani supported Hart's proposal. During the first week of the police crackdown, more than fifteen hundred people were arrested and questioned. The vast majority were African American males. Commissioner Hart stated that he was pleased with the campaign's progress despite the fact that many of those arrested were "taken into custody after being stopped on the street as suspicious persons." In other words, police had a free reign to round up black men, even if there was no evidence that they were guilty. African Americans were infuriated at the randomness of this sweep. One prominent black UAW leader complained that "any Negro standing on the corner, coming out of the house to get in his car, going to the church, going into a store, coming out of a store, going into a nightclub or coming out of a nightclub" was likely to face harassment and arrest.[66]

Angry and frustrated, the black community helped elect Jerome Cavanagh, a young, little-known liberal, to the mayor's office in 1961. After his surprising victory, Cavanagh promised to improve relations between African Americans and the Detroit Police. He ordered the city to institute nondiscriminatory hiring practices, which would force the virtually all-white police department to hire African Americans. He appointed George Edwards, the liberal who had been defeated by Cobo in 1949, as police commissioner and gave him a mandate to change the department.

As liberals fought to reform the police department, crime became an increasingly important issue for white conservatives. An editorial on one local television station summed up the attitude of many conservatives toward Cavangh's reforms: "We don't like the sound of it. The city must be protected, and the police must have the full backing in doing their job, or the community one day might have to go back to the law of the jungle." In 1965, the wife of one white policeman wrote to Cavanagh asking that he not "further weaken the protection of Detroit's citizens against the daily rapes, robberies, knifings and murders by lawless members of the Negro community. . . . With the black man's switchblade at their throats, the white community wants a strong, resolute force of well-trained police officers."[67] Rather than seeing police brutality as a violation of constitutional rights, white conservatives argued that liberal attempts to restrict police power endangered the community. While conservatives supported limited government when they discussed housing, their attitude toward police power was quite different. Only a large and strong police force, they argued, stood between the white community and supposedly rapacious, violent African Americans.

Fair Employment

Fair employment was the third major issue that racial liberals sought to solve during the late 1940s and 1950s. As in the debate over desegregated housing, civil rights supporters faced a great deal of opposition from conservatives in their attempts to break the color line. Despite their efforts, activists achieved relatively little success during the early postwar period. Fair-employment practice regulations in the defense industry during World War II had given blacks an entrée into well-paid manufacturing jobs that had previously been closed to them. The UAW acted forcefully against white workers who walked off the job and refused to work with African Americans during World War II. After the war, the liberal civil-rights coalition fought for fair employment practices legislation in hopes that removing job restrictions would allow blacks to further the gains they had made. However, by the end of 1945, according to UAW estimates, more than half of black wartime workers were laid off. This effectively brought the number of African Americans in the auto industry back to pre–World War II levels. While the UAW leadership supported fair employment, many UAW locals returned to their prewar discriminatory practices. During the war, for example, hundreds of black workers in the Hamtramck Dodge Main plant were upgraded to semiskilled classifications. Shortly after the war, white workers once again staffed the departments in Dodge Main almost exclusively. UAW Local 3, the Dodge Main local, reinstituted its prewar seniority program, which gave seniority on a department-by-department basis. This meant that a black foundry worker, for example, would lose his seniority if he moved to a different department. Such a policy kept black workers in unskilled jobs and helped keep auto plants segregated.[68]

Thus, after the war, black employment gains appeared threatened, as discriminatory hiring became increasingly common. The number of employment notices that explicitly limited jobs to "whites only" increased by 80 percent in some Michigan State Employment Service offices between 1946 and 1950. By November 1950, one branch office reported that nonwhites had filed 47.5 percent of the unemployment compensation applications while only 15 percent of the available jobs were opened to them. In the auto industry, the largest employer in the Detroit area, hiring was highly decentralized and done largely at the discretion of the local plant manager. This led to large variations in hiring practices, even within the city of Detroit. Some managers, who were loath to disrupt "traditionally" white plants, refused to consider black job applications. The African Americans who were hired were once again restricted to the dirtiest, most dangerous, and least desirable jobs.[69] White autoworkers also played a crucial role in maintaining the color line. According to historian Kevin Boyle, "White rank and filers insisted that they had the right to determine the sort of person they worked beside, a right they protected through the workplace action that had been the hallmark of the early UAW." They exerted their control locally on the shop floor and regionally through their union. Both workers and management thus played a key role in many plants in keeping the shop floor white.[70]

While the union leadership had moved forcefully during the war against the racist hate strikes, they embraced a more gradualist approach after the war. UAW President Walter Reuther claimed that, on the issue of race, "the leadership had progressed faster than the rank and file." This belief shaped his policy of gradualism, particularly in the South. Publicly, Reuther blamed management for discriminatory hiring and claimed that the union had no power to change management's employment policies.[71] However, the UAW leadership was rarely as forceful as black activists wanted them to be. While Reuther and the UAW leadership were well known for their support of civil rights nationally, they were reluctant to move forcefully against white union members who supported segregation. While the leadership was willing to ally with black activists, their goals differed. As historian David Lewis-Colman has argued, "Black activists' primary question was how to advance black rights and freedom, while the primary question that guided the civil rights politics of the UAW's white leaders was how to handle 'racial problems' without destroying unions."[72]

African Americans found it particularly hard to break into the skilled trades. The UAW leadership had little desire to challenge the color line in the powerful trades since doing so would deprive the skilled workers of their right to control entry into their craft. Skilled autoworkers successfully resisted union attempts to desegregate their trades during the 1950s. In 1951, for example, the UAW's Fair Practices Department sent two black apprentices to the Detroit Fleetwood plant. White workers struck in protest, which led the union to remove the two. A few years later, the union attempted to include African Americans in the city's all-white apprenticeship programs. Once again the skilled tradesmen resisted, and the union backed down.[73]

In the midst of such unsuccessful attempts to achieve fair employment, a Communist-led organization called the Greater Detroit Labor Council began a campaign to place a fair employment practices referendum on the city ballot. The ordinance that the left-wing coalition proposed was identical to the legislation that liberals supported on the state level. But, while liberals backed the language of the 1951 left-wing bill, they did not endorse the idea of a municipal referendum. They recognized that such legislation would be largely symbolic, especially since it would not cover Highland Park, Dearborn, or any of the key industrial areas outside of the city. The liberal coalition that formed in response to the referendum campaign, called the Detroit Citizens Committee for Equal Employment Opportunities, refused to work with any Communist Party front groups and strongly attacked the leftist referendum drive. The Citizens Committee feared that the Communists were highlighting discriminatory hiring practices to gain propaganda points and increase their stature in the black and labor communities. "As a matter of fact," a Citizens Committee memo stated, "the CP policy now seems to be to exploit the misery of the Negro population to win the loyalty of minority citizens and then use that loyalty to try to recapture power in the labor movement." Committee members particularly worried that the Communists would use the issue to capture the powerful UAW Local 600, which had a large and politically active black membership. The committee also feared that the Communists sought a referendum in order to stir up hate groups. "Organizations which sell hate for profit will set up business in Detroit just as they did in California, Tucson, Arizona and Oregon in times past," the committee warned. "FEPC has never won in a referendum vote anywhere in America. Bigots and misinformed citizens have always been stirred up. Feelings mount. Tension grows. Just one group gets anything out of it—the Communist Party and its front membership organizations. Frightened minority citizens easily turn to a strong arm, ostensibly friendly organization in time of crisis." The committee did not want "to see Detroit invaded by race hate groups and soaked with bad racial feeling."[74] The committee feared that the referendum would encourage fair employment opponents to associate FEP with Communism, thus leading them to discredit the idea as illegitimate.

The liberal coalition won their battle against the front group: the fair employment practices referendum was kept off the local ballot. However, segregation in employment remained a pressing problem in the African American community. In the wake of the referendum battle, liberals worried that segregationists now had more ammunition to use in their assertion that the fight for civil rights was a Communist campaign.

Shortly after the referendum defeat, the House Un-American Activities Committee (HUAC) came to Detroit to investigate Communism in the defense industry. The committee particularly targeted UAW Local 600, the large, heavily African American, left-led local at Ford's River Rouge plant that had been at the forefront of the fight for fair employment. Delegates from Local 600 had been the ones who called on the UAW to create a Fair Practices Department in 1943. During the early 1950s, radicals in Local 600 were at the forefront in fighting against the automation and decentralization that the auto companies sought. Because they lacked seniority, black Ford workers were disproportionately targeted by this decentralization policy and thus were especially critical of company policy.[75] In the midst of the local's high-profile battle with Ford, HUAC subpoenaed a number of prominent black leftists, including William Hood, Local 600's recording secretary and national chairman of the National Negro Labor Council; Arthur McPhaul, Executive Secretary of the Civil Rights Congress of Michigan and Ford pressed steel worker; Shelton Tappes, former president of the foundry unit of Local 600's; Nelson Davis, vice-president of the Rouge's foundry workers; and Coleman Young, former Ford worker and national executive secretary of the National Negro Labor Council. In addition, the committee called Rev. Charles Hill, a Baptist minister and prominent civil rights activist who had worked closely with Communists on a number of campaigns.

Many of the black militants forcefully defied HUAC and portrayed themselves as civil rights fighters rather than subversives. Coleman Young denounced segregation and stated that he thought it was significant that the committee "single[d] out Negro leaders who have been fighting for Negro equality."[76] Rev. Charles Hill responded to a congressman who questioned how a "man of the cloth" could assist Communists by insisting that he did not ask anyone about their religious or political beliefs. Instead, Hill stated, "I have been interested in primarily one thing, and that is discrimination, segregation, the second-class citizenship my people suffer, and as long as I live, until it is eradicated from this American society, I will accept the cooperation of anybody who wants to make America the land of the free and the home of the brave."[77]

Black liberals were largely silent on the subject of HUAC's hearings. The *Michigan Chronicle*, for instance, gave only a brief mention of the fact that the committee had subpoenaed prominent African American radicals. The paper did not reprint either Reverend Hill's defiant statement or Coleman Young's fiery denunciation of HUAC's racism. Nor did it discuss any of the threatened lynchings or effigy hangings that occurred in Detroit factories.[78] The editors of the *Chronicle* did not complain when the International Executive Board of the UAW, in the wake of HUAC testimony that highlighted Communist power in Local 600, seized control of the Ford local and placed it under administratorship on March 12. "The Negro workers at the Ford Motor Company should feel that the International has done them a service by clearing the air within the official life of the Ford Motor Company," Reverend White proclaimed. "There are many problems facing the Negro workers at the Ford Plant which could never get an honest consideration as long as the Union was under American Communist domination. The Communists will and have always used the problems that confront Negroes to attempt to advance Communism. . . . The Negro is only a pawn whenever the Communists start working with the problems."[79] Despite the Local's long history of fighting for fair employment practices, black liberals supported HUAC in order to purge the civil rights movement of Communists.

After the HUAC hearings, Detroit Communists found themselves largely on the defensive. They spent much of their time fighting against government lawsuits rather than engaging in civil rights campaigns. Liberal activists continued to fight for an FEP law, and they won a significant victory when the state of Michigan passed an FEP law in 1955. While the law was important symbolically, it gave the state little power to enforce fair employment. The FEPC committee that the law established could only respond to complaints that workers brought before it. It had no ability to fight against the exclusion of African Americans from certain types of employment. As a result, the law, according to one historian, "made a tiny dent in a major problem."[80]

During the late 1950s, some prominent black UAW activists became frustrated with the union's failure to make a significant impact on segregation in employment. Inspired by the civil-rights activism in the South, the activists created the Trade Union Leadership Council (TULC) to address the issues black workers faced in both the workplace and in their unions. These men were exasperated at the UAW's seeming unwillingness to improve black workers' status in local factories. While African Americans made up almost 20 percent of the workforce in Detroit's auto plants, they held less than 1 percent of the skilled jobs and 40 percent of the low-level laborer positions.[81] The TULC also challenged the UAW hierarchy, which had refused to sit an African American on the union's International Executive Board. During the 1959 UAW convention, Horace Sheffield, one of the founders of the TULC, denounced the union's hypocrisy and insisted that black workers could no longer "accept as adequate the fact that some of our international unions have a good public posture on the question of 'civil rights and fair practices' while, at the same time, they resist with every means at their disposal any effort to change the 'lily-white' character of their own international executive boards."[82] Thus, by the end of the 1950s, African-American activists were coming into conflict with their white liberal allies on the subject of employment. For much of the decade, African American activists had reluctantly complied with the gradualism of the UAW leadership. However, as African Americans found themselves still locked out of the skilled trades and still confined to some of the worst jobs in auto plants, they began challenging the liberal gradualist strategy.

The TULC was at the forefront of the movement to defeat Mayor Miriani and elect Jerome Cavanaugh in 1961. Their main focus, however, was on jobs and job discrimination. They helped develop a coalition of local civil rights groups that fought against discrimination in apprenticeship programs, in the skilled trades, in the automobile industry, in downtown Detroit retail stores, and in government employment. In 1963, they issued an ultimatum to Mayor Cavanaugh that gave unions and employers thirty days to make a commitment to integration. If integration did not occur, the coalition promised to take direct action "in the tradition of Birmingham."[83] While TULC achieved some success, black nationalism and student revolutionaries increasingly influenced some black autoworkers during the mid- and late 1960s. By the late 1960s, new, more radical civil-rights organizations, called Revolutionary Union Movements (RUMs) appeared in Detroit's auto plants. While their ideology was far more militant than TULC's, they, like the earlier civil-rights organization, dedicated themselves to fighting racism in the auto plants.

Such assertiveness on the part of northern African Americans angered many white autoworkers. Whites at the Ypsilanti, Michigan, Ford factory burned a cross on the plant's lawn to demonstrate against African American "aggressiveness."[84] By 1965, a survey of white autoworkers in Michigan found that 32 percent believed that the civil-rights movement was moving too quickly. By 1967, another poll found that half of white autoworkers opposed further integration. Detroit-area autoworkers increasingly linked what was happening in the city's neighborhoods to the protests in the factories. As historian Heather Thompson argued, as white fear of blacks on the assembly line increased, "they refused to concede the possible legitimacy of both African American shop-floor complaints and black grievances in the city." To conservative white workers, "black 'rebellion' in either the plants or on city streets was merely an excuse for engaging in racially motivated violence."[85] By 1968, entire UAW locals were supporting George Wallace's candidacy for president to express their opposition to integration on the shop floor as well as the neighborhood.

Conclusion

The story of racial conflict in 1960s Detroit is well known. However, as we have seen, African American demands for integrated housing, the end to police brutality, and fair employment began far earlier. So did the development of a conservative response to black campaigns. White opponents argued that Communists were behind the fight for civil rights. They complained that desegregation in housing and employment would hurt property values and deprive whites of their right to decide whom they wanted to work with. As liberalism became increasingly concerned with racial matters during the 1940s, liberals found that their racial rhetoric often alienated white working-class homeowners. The latter group instead turned to politicians like Albert Cobo, who championed small government, which meant protecting home, family, and neighborhood from integration. These voters ignored the hypocrisy inherent in their support of antistatism as they continued to embrace popular welfare-state policies like FHA guaranteed home loans.[86]

The racial debate that occurred in Detroit during the late 1940s and early 1950s made it quite clear that no liberal consensus for integration existed amongst Detroit's whites. In fact, according to a large-scale study undertaken in 1952, 68 percent of white respondents proposed that the city deal with its racial problems through some form of segregation. As one interviewee stated, "Negroes [are] all right in [their] own place. Honestly I prefer the way they handle it down South. They keep to themselves and don't live in your [white] part of town. Let them keep to themselves if you ask me." Almost a decade after the 1943 riot and the subsequent attempts to ameliorate racial conflict, Detroit whites in 1952 supported segregation at higher rates than they had in 1942. Nor were UAW members, whose union had repeatedly attempted to educate workers on racial matters, any different from non-UAW members in their willingness to accept African Americans.[87] The racial conflict often associated with the South during the 1960s occurred in Detroit during the late 1940s and 1950s. The ideology that developed out of this conflict— antistatism—would later be a key component of modern conservatism.

CHAPTER FOUR

ANTI-COMMUNISM AND CATHOLICISM IN COLD-WAR DETROIT

On May 1, 1947, more than five thousand men met on a sidewalk in front of a church in downtown Detroit just as office workers were leaving for the day. At 5:00 P.M., the men knelt, despite the driving rain, and began to pray the rosary. These members of the Detroit Archdiocesan Council of Catholic Men complained that "Socialists, atheistic Communists . . . [and] votaries of the Red Antichrist" had made so much "noise and clamor" on May Day that it had come to be a Communist holiday. May 1, they protested, had become the day when radicals "roared forth their false gospel of materialism, [and] chanted their atheistic anthems." In the process, they had "drowned out the hymns that exalted Mary." In response, these men vowed to "Make May Day Mary's Day." As they knelt in the rain, clutching their rosaries, these Catholics were determined to "return Russia to the Heart of Christ."[1]

Northern urban Catholics were some of the devoted supporters of the Democratic Party and the New Deal. Yet, during the second half of the twentieth century, Catholics played what one scholar has portrayed as an "irreplaceable part" in the modern conservative movement.[2] Why did this transition from liberal to conservative occur within the Catholic community? While the battles against abortion during the 1970s and 1980s were important, Catholic conservatism developed earlier, in the 1940s and 1950s. We see the beginnings of Catholic conservatism in public devotions like the one above. Catholic conservatism developed out of fears that the United States was becoming Godless. Secularism, many Catholics believed, was the true danger the nation and the Western world faced. This was why the Catholic men on the sidewalk in downtown Detroit embraced prayer as their weapon of choice. Communism, Catholics argued, developed in the "fertile soil" of secularism. Catholics during the 1940s and 1950s thus expressed two crucial elements of modern conservatism—anti-Communism and traditionalism. They argued that Communism, by emphasizing the material nature of humans, denied the spiritual essence of man. While American Catholics certainly recognized the strategic threat the Soviet Union presented, Catholic opposition to secularism and "Godless Communism" did not develop in response to this danger and predated the Cold War. Instead, it developed out of a fear that Communism threatened the Church, and the increasingly secular nature of American society made the nation hostile to spiritual values. Catholics wanted to preserve the church's ancient moral traditions and impart these values into American society.

Catholic Anti-Communism before the Cold War

Catholic opposition to Communism began long before the Cold War. During the nineteenth century, church leaders worried that the rise of Marxism both in Europe and in the United States threatened Catholicism, particularly among the working class. As a result, the church hierarchy in the late nineteenth and early twentieth centuries crafted a critique of industrialization that condemned both the brutal conditions industrialism created for workers and the Marxist solution to the labor problem.[3] Pope Pius XI, for example, insisted that workers had to be paid sufficient wages to support their families and asserted, "If this cannot always be done under existing circumstances, social justice demands that changes be introduced as soon as possible whereby such a wage will be assured to every adult workingman."[4] However, he simultaneously condemned "bolshevistic and atheistic Communism . . . [which] aims at upsetting the social order and at undermining the very foundations of Christian civilization." The Pope explicitly linked atheism and Communism in his portrayal of the latter, which, he argued, emphasized materialism and denied the existence of spirit. Communism, according to the church, threatened the "very idea of God."[5]

During the 1930s, these papal messages were popularized throughout Detroit and the rest of the nation in the early radio sermons of Father Charles Coughlin, best known now for his protofascist anti-Semitism. As the Depression ravaged the Detroit area, Coughlin took to the airways to condemn both Communism and predatory capitalism. "The thoughtful American," the priest argued, was convinced that "the most dangerous communist is the wolf in the sheep's clothing of conservatism who is bent upon preserving the

policies of greed, of oppression and of Christlessness."[6] In the early years
of the Depression, capitalism, not Communism, posed the greater threat
according to Coughlin.

However, the Spanish Civil War, along with highly publicized Bolshevik
atrocities against Catholics in Mexico and the Soviet Union during the
1930s, convinced many Catholics that Communism rather than laissez-faire
capitalism presented the greater danger. Catholic newspapers trumpeted
Spanish Republican atrocities committed against the church—priests and
nuns slaughtered, churches and tombs desecrated, and monasteries sacked.
The Catholic hierarchy argued that Communist actions in Spain showed
that "for the first time in history we are witnessing a struggle, cold blooded
in purpose and mapped out to the last detail between man and 'all that is
called God.'"[7] Communists, according to this view, wanted to destroy the
church and replace Catholicism with an ideology that lacked all moral re-
straint. Church leaders portrayed Catholics and Communists as locked in
a Manichean battle that would not end until one or the other was defeated.

As a result of Communist atrocities, by the late 1930s, Father Coughlin's
anti-Communism became so strident and so profascist that it began to drown
out the more prolabor elements of his earlier rhetoric. Coughlin turned
against the CIO, which he claimed was riddled with Communists. Coughlin's
blatant anti-Semitism, criticism of Franklin Roosevelt, and condemnation of
the CIO deprived the priest of much of the enormous audience, including
many Catholics, he enjoyed during the early New Deal. Those followers
who continued to support him often did so because he alone seemed to them
to be standing up against international Communism, which both Coughlin
and his listeners increasingly viewed as a Jewish conspiracy. In a November
1938 radio address, Coughlin alleged that Jews had been largely responsible
for the Russian revolution and were to blame for the spread of Communism
through the world. In a typical apology for fascism, Coughlin claimed that
Nazism, while deplorable, had to be understood "as a defense mechanism
against the incursions of Communism."[8]

Coughlin's supporters during this period expressed some key elements that
would later be apparent in postwar Catholic conservatism: hatred of Communism as a materialistic and atheistic philosophy that was incompatible
with Christianity, anger at Communist persecution of Catholics overseas,
and belief that subversives within the American government conspired to
weaken the nation's resolve to fight Communism abroad. Letters written
to Coughlin during this period were filled with these themes. For example,
Vance Marran of Detroit argued that Coughlin's critics unfairly accused
him of anti-Semitism solely so they could "nullify his great work in expos-

ing communism and its causes as well as its authors hidden and known. The God-Haters and the Power-Worshippers, through a controlled radio and press, want Father Coughlin silenced so that they can without fear of exposure clasp the gory hands of those fresh dipped in the blood of Catholic martyrs in Spain and elsewhere."[9] Thus, well before the Cold War began, Catholics were steeped in anti-Communism and anti-Communist language. They articulated an ideology that, during this period, had virtually nothing to do with any strategic threat the Soviet Union presented to the United States. Instead, Catholic anti-Communists vehemently insisted that they alone recognized the danger Communists posed to Christianity and the Christian morality that was the basis for Western society.[10]

The Hierarchy's Response

During the late 1930s, Coughlin's condemnation of the CIO and his apology for Nazism presented problems for the Detroit archdiocese. While the hierarchy shared Coughlin's abhorrence toward the Communist Party, they feared that he might be undermining workingmen's Catholicism. The working class in Detroit was heavily Catholic. Archbishop Edward Mooney, the newly installed leader of the Detroit archdiocese, worried that a whole generation of men might leave the church if they believed the hierarchy was allied with employers and hostile to legitimate unions. While Mooney was inexcusably slow to condemn Coughlin's anti-Semitism, he was quick to silence Coughlin's attacks on the CIO.[11] Shortly after he took office, the archbishop refused to provide his imprimatur for a pamphlet titled "Can Christians Join the CIO?" that Coughlin planned to publish, because he feared that the work would "stir up unnecessary and unduly bitter strife among Catholics in a matter of critical importance to our workingmen." Mooney wanted Catholic workers to join the CIO both to improve their economic status and to act as a moderating force in the new labor movement against Communists.[12]

In order to appeal to Catholic workers, Mooney threw his support behind the Association of Catholic Trade Unionists (ACTU), a labor group that sought to be a "real power for the Cause of Christ in the labor movement." ACTU's goals were twofold: first, to "carry the message of trade unionism into every working-class Catholic home" and, second, to "carry the gospel of Christianity into every labor union."[13] ACTU was a means for the church to show support for the CIO while also pushing Communists out of the unions. In addition, the archbishop began the Archdiocesan Labor Institute in 1939. The institute sponsored parish labor schools, which taught workers about the corporatist philosophy of the papal encyclicals and about parliamentary procedure. The schools were particularly effective in achieving the latter goal. Workers who filled out surveys in the early labor schools noted that their classes gave them "more confidence to speak" and enabled them to "ask for things that I think we need." Learning parliamentary procedures helped these Catholic workers battle against Communists in union meetings. The labor schools, in conjunction with ACTU, helped create a Catholic "caucus within a caucus" in unions. This paralleled the role that Communist fractions played in unions and helped Catholic minorities push Communist minorities out of power in some local unions and labor organizations.[14] Detroit ACTU achieved a major victory during the war when it helped drive a Communist-left group out of the Michigan CIO. By the late 1940s, ACTU and other Catholic liberals were a small but prominent group within the Detroit UAW. Labor schools and the labor priests who ran them represented the liberal wing of Catholicism. They viewed government as a positive force for social reform and believed they could teach workers how to drive Communists out of the labor movement.[15]

Catholicism and American Foreign Policy

Anti-Communism remained a major concern for American Catholics during World War II despite the United States' alliance with the Soviet Union. During the war, the Catholic press in the United States trumpeted the idea that Communists sought to destroy the church. This steady anti-Soviet drumbeat received relatively little support from Protestant denominations or the secular media. During the war, the church's anti-Communist focus switched from Spain to Soviet actions in Eastern Europe, particularly Poland. In early 1944, at a time when the mainstream American media shied away from anti-Soviet articles, the *Michigan Catholic* and other diocesan papers regularly criticized Soviet activities in Poland and insisted that the Soviet Union continued to persecute the Catholic Church. They dismissed the Popular Front idea that Stalin was allowing greater freedom of religion and contended that Russia wanted Poland.[16] Even before V-E day, editors and columnists in the *Michigan Catholic* warned their readers that the Soviets sought to move the postwar Polish-Soviet border west to the old Curzon line. This would mean that Poland would lose 46 percent of its prewar territory. In return, the Soviets wanted to move the Polish-German border west to the Oder River, thus taking land away from Germany and giving it to Poland. A *Michigan Catholic* editorial warned that if Poland were reconstituted along the borders the Soviets wanted, it would be so weak that it would be easily "submerged and overcome by the Communist flood." In addition, a "dismembered Germany" and a "weakened France" would not be able to withstand the Communist deluge. "And what had long ago been the dream of the Mongol tribes and of the Turk," the editors warned, "shall at last become a reality: the Christendom of Europe shall be terribly crippled if not utterly destroyed."[17] While the mainstream American press was filled with articles about Soviet cooperation with the Allies, the Catholic media warned of Communist duplicity in the traditional territories of Russian imperialism and depicted the church as the crucial protector of Western civilization.

Such warnings helped fracture the previously united Slavic community in the Detroit area at the end of the war. Eastern Europeans, especially Poles, constituted a large percentage of the Detroit immigrant population and were particularly prevalent in industrial areas such as Hamtramck (home of the enormous Dodge Main plant) and Detroit's east side.[18] Poles had their own Polish-language newspapers, radio programs, and meeting halls. During the 1930s, pro-Soviet labor activists had been able to work within the larger Slavic-American community. Leftist Poles such as Stanley Nowak played a key role in organizing their fellow Eastern European workers in the UAW and other CIO unions. Conservative Polish priests and businessmen were often hostile to the CIO's unionization efforts, which they believed were Communist-led. Despite this opposition, many Eastern European workers overlooked their organizers' politics throughout the Depression. Stanley Nowak, for example, was able to parlay Polish support into a seat in the Michigan Senate from 1938 to 1947, despite the relentless red baiting he faced. Immigrant organizations opened their meeting halls to the fledgling UAW during the early years of unionization, and Polish groups from across the political spectrum came together in 1941 to write a manifesto in support of the UAW's organizing drive at Ford.[19]

This alliance of Detroit's Eastern Europeans continued during the war under the American Slav Congress, which united Slavic immigrants behind the war effort and encouraged cooperation between the United States, eastern European homelands, and the Soviet Union. During the months after V-E Day, many Detroit Poles downplayed their political differences in order to help the Polish recovery. For example, when a delegation led by Stanley Nowak traveled to Poland immediately after the war, they ran into another group led by Bishop Stephan Woznicki of Detroit. The two groups met and compared notes over dinner almost every night. They agreed that they would not broach any politically controversial subjects once they returned to Detroit but would instead focus on gaining aid for Poland. This agreement helped set the tone for a series of dispatches written by Philip Adler, a reporter from the *Detroit News*, who described the horrific physical condition of postwar Warsaw while largely downplaying the political situation.[20]

However, Soviet activities in Poland made this alliance difficult to maintain. When the Allies agreed at Yalta to adopt the Curzon line as Poland's eastern boundary, leaders of Detroit's Eastern European community almost unanimously expressed their dissatisfaction. Janusz Ostrowski, editor of the *Polish Daily News (Dziennik Polski)*, stated, "[I was] greatly surprised and disappointed because I believe Poland has been cheated awfully bad."[21] After the Potsdam conference, Ostrowski insisted that the "majority" of Polish-Americans in Michigan opposed the Potsdam agreement and that only a few (presumably pro-Soviet Poles) favored it.[22] Not surprisingly, a number of articles in the local Catholic newspaper warned of increasing Soviet persecution. Walter Dushnyck, a Ukrainian-American who wrote a series of articles based on his interviews with two unnamed Ukrainian Catholic priests, claimed that "the Catholic Church, even more than democracy as such, is recognized as a deadly opponent to the Soviet system in its drive to the west. Consequently, in the Soviet Union and in all Soviet-occupied countries, we find a vast, government-sponsored and directed movement against the Catholic Church and the Vatican."[23] Many Slavic-Americans argued that the Soviets endangered both the Catholic Church and their various homelands, and they often joined the two threats in their anti-Soviet language. As Communism became associated with both Russian imperialism and anti-Catholic violence, numerous Detroit Eastern Europeans turned against their former allies on the left. After Michigan Governor Kim Sigler named Stanley Nowak as a Communist sympathizer during his HUAC testimony in March 1947, the previously popular Nowak found that he could not be elected to the Detroit Common Council in 1947 or to Congress in 1948. By 1952, when Nowak chaired a banquet in honor of Polish Ambassador Jozef Winiewicz, the division within the Eastern European community was so sharp that no Polish organization would rent out its hall for the dinner.[24]

The Catholic Church thus increasingly became a locus for Slavic-American protests against the Soviets during the mid-1940s. Church leaders regularly spoke in favor of free elections in Eastern Europe. In a mass held in front of two thousand people in Blessed Sacrament Cathedral on Polish Constitution Day, Archbishop Mooney stated, "The treatment accorded to Poland will determine whether we shall have real peace or merely another armistice."[25] Catholic newspapers were filled with gruesome depictions of mass deportations of Poles and brutalities committed against Lithuanian, Slovenian, and Ukrainian Catholics. These criticisms of Soviet policies in

Eastern Europe proved popular among many Slavs in Detroit. As Arthur I. Zakrzewski of Hamtramck wrote in a letter to the editor, "The Poles of Detroit know that The *Michigan Catholic* is doing a splendid job in printing the truth about Poland."[26]

In many ways, the language Catholics used to describe Soviet persecution of the church in Eastern Europe resembled their late-1930s warnings about Spain. However, Catholic support of Franco made the church vulnerable to charges that it was antidemocratic and profascist. But when the Knights of Columbus passed an anti-Communist resolution in 1946, they pointed out that the Soviets "had violated the ideals expressed in the Atlantic Charter for which the United States fought in World War II."[27] Catholic anti-Communist warnings during the mid-1940s thus positioned the church as a defender of American foreign policy ideals, not as a profascist apologist. As a result, Catholic anti-Communist criticism received a far more sympathetic hearing in the mid-1940s than it had during the Spanish Civil War.[28]

Communist actions in Eastern Europe caused a great deal of concern for the Catholic hierarchy in the United States and caused them to change the Church's focus, particularly in the labor arena. While the papal encyclicals had critiqued both unrestrained capitalism and Communism, Catholics in 1944 and 1945 began shifting the emphasis of their activities solely toward anti-Communism in the wake of Soviet activities. The continuing power of Communists within the CIO, particularly the CIO Political Action Committee (CIO-PAC), also pushed some labor priests in a more conservative direction. By late 1944, when Fr. John Cronin was appointed to write an extensive study of Communism in America, the church had moved toward an "unrelenting war on CIO Communists," in the words of one historian. Everything, including the church's critique of capitalism, was subordinated to the anti-Communist struggle. By 1945, Catholic liberals found themselves increasingly out of step with the church hierarchy.

Traditionalism

Catholic anti-Communism in Detroit was not confined to Slavic-Americans, and its expression extended well beyond resolutions and letters to the editor. Many Catholics in Detroit, like Catholics in other major cities, participated in large and enthusiastic popular devotions, many of which were explicitly anti-Communist.[29] This devotional culture, which was central to both the everyday life and the religious practice of American Catholics before Vatican II, has been largely invisible to historians of American society and politics. For many Catholics, secularism was the crucial problem faced by

American society. Communism, they argued, developed in the "fertile soil" of secularism. Their hostility to the former was in fact part of a much larger opposition to the latter.[30]

One of the most popular Catholic devotions during the 1940s and 1950s was the Rosary prayed to Our Lady of Fatima.[31] This practice had its roots in an apparition of the Virgin Mary that purportedly appeared to three peasant children in Fatima, Portugal, in 1917. Mary told them, "If people do what I have told you, many souls will be saved and will find peace. If people do not cease to offend God, not much time will elapse, and precisely in the next pontificate, another and more terrible war will commence." To avoid another conflict, Mary made three requests: Catholics should consecrate the world to her Immaculate Heart, receive Communion in reparation on the first Saturday of each month, and pray the Rosary for the conversion of Russia. According to the peasant children, Mary claimed,

> If my requests are granted, Russia will be converted; there will be peace. Otherwise, Russia will spread its errors throughout the world, giving rise to wars and persecutions against the Church. The good will suffer martyrdom and the Holy Father will have to suffer much. Different nations will be destroyed. But in the end my Immaculate Heart will triumph. The Holy Father will consecrate Russia to the Immaculate Heart and Russia will be converted and an era of peace will be given to the world.[32]

The Church provided official sanction to the Fatima devotion during World War II when Pius XII consecrated the world—and Russia in particular—to the Immaculate Heart of Mary. As a result, many Catholics believed that they could now "invoke her aid and trust that again she will intervene and never permit the Cross to be supplanted by the Hammer and the Sickle."[33]

While Marian devotions could be explicitly anti-Communist, they also allowed devotees to express a complex set of fears while providing spiritual solace. One of the most popular forms of Marian devotion in Detroit, the block Rosary, began in 1944 when an anonymous Detroit housewife, worried about the safety of her brothers in the military, had a vision of the Virgin.[34] The housewife's recounting of this visitation is filled with a sense of loss and sorrow. One brother had already been killed in the war, and she longed to secure the safety of her remaining six brothers in the battlefield. She began praying a Novena and was almost instantly given a sense of comfort. "[A]s I recited each Rosary, it seemed so beautiful that I wished to remain on my knees, and as I finished each one, I gave it to OUR BLESSED MOTHER AS THOUGH SHE WERE STANDING BEFORE ME. Then the thought came to me, 'I have nothing to worry about. My brothers are safe.'"

Her sense of security lasted until the battle of Iwo Jima, when she became overwhelmed with a feeling that one brother's life was at stake. In a panic, she vowed to donate more blood, buy more bonds, and save more scrap. She suddenly heard a voice that said "YOUR BLOOD WILL NOT SAVE YOUR BROTHER. YOUR BONDS WILL NOT SAVE HIM. YOUR TIN CANS AND YOUR PAPER WILL NOT SAVE HIM." Mary then appeared to the housewife looking "as though a thousand swords were piercing HER heart." She showed the housewife a vision of grey-haired women on their knees in a circle, and "in their faces was such bitter grief as if each had a son who was about to be hanged, and that GOD alone could save him. Then I saw a bomb coming through the roof, and again it appeared as though only GOD's hand could stop it. That was the only hope." The Virgin told the housewife that the women she saw were praying the rosary and said, "WHEREVER THESE GROUPS WILL GATHER, I WILL GIVE THEM PROTECTION. I SHALL BLESS THEIR HOMES. I WILL BE IN THEIR MIDST." She urged the housewife, "TAKE THEM THE FIRST WEEK; ANOTHER THE NEXT, ETC. ONCE A WEEK, TIME, 7:30 P.M. HOUSE BY HOUSE; STREET BY STREET." The housewife responded repeatedly "NO, BLESSED MOTHER, I can't; I'm no good. I'm unworthy." Mary ordered her to go, and she did. She knocked on her neighbors' doors, and thus began the first block Rosary group.[35] For this housewife, Mary's message was clear—prayer, not worldly actions, would provide protection.

This apparition was an intensely personal religious experience between the devout Catholic housewife and the Virgin Mary.[36] However, the practice that grew out of this visitation quickly grew in scope and developed new meanings for its practitioners. Nicholas Schorn, a retired Detroit businessman, popularized the spiritual and antisecular message of this Marian apparition. Schorn believed that "the main reason the world is going to the devil is because it has abandoned God. I want to help to save the world through real peace and to keep America Christian." Schorn, like many other Catholics, believed that American society was in crisis, largely because it had fallen away from traditional Catholic values in its move toward secular liberalism.[37] Like other traditionalists, Schorn rejected the liberal idea that society could be understood through reasoned analysis and perfected by rational policies. Liberalism, he believed, ignored original sin. By rejecting this idea, society turned its back on the church's teachings and disregarded the inherently sinful and flawed nature of mankind.

Schorn urged Catholics to vanquish secular liberalism by interjecting their beliefs into the public sphere. He argued that the Rosary was the most potent weapon Catholics had to accomplish this goal. He pointed out that

"Mary, the Mother of God, possesses the most intimate contact with divinity.
... At her intercession, Jesus, before His time, performed his first public
miracle. This remarkable example of Her maternal authority plainly tells
us that we have a powerful Mother in Heaven, from whom Jesus will not
turn His face when she pleads for Her children." When Mary's followers
prayed the Rosary in the manner she had requested, Schorn stressed, Mary
would intercede with Jesus and grant her followers' wishes.[38]

Marian devotions were enormously popular among lay Catholics in Detroit. The 1947 campaign to "Make May Day Mary's Day" was only one
of many such public devotions. When the Detroit Archdiocesan Council of
Catholic Men prayed their Rosaries, they seized control of a public space
in downtown Detroit to assert their opposition both to Soviet actions and
to the primacy of secular, socialist values in the public sphere. This yearly
assembly continued to draw between three thousand and ten thousand
celebrants every May 1 until 1958.[39]

An even larger lay devotion was held in the University of Detroit football
stadium every May. These yearly ceremonies seamlessly combined Catholicism and patriotism as the Knights of Columbus, the National Guard, school
bands, and sodalities joined with the church hierarchy in a day of proces-
sions, Rosaries for the conversion of Russia, the saying of the Pledge of Allegiance, and singing of the Star Spangled Banner. Members of the different
groups came together to form an enormous, living Rosary on the football
field and watched as one lucky Catholic girl who had been named "Queen
of the Day" crowned the Virgin's statue. This devotion proved so popular
that in 1954, one hundred thousand people attended while thousands more
watched on television or listened on the radio.[40] Through these large public
devotions, Catholics interjected their cultural values in the public sphere in
order to influence the larger urban culture of Detroit. These devotionalists
contested the messages that other groups, like the CPUSA, expressed in the
streets of Detroit in their protests and marches.

As they practiced these devotions, Catholics expressed a complex ideology.
While they opposed Soviet foreign policy in Eastern Europe, their larger
focus was secularism. Catholics feared that, by excluding God from their
thinking and living, Americans were losing the foundation for their moral
values. Communism could easily develop in the "fertile soil" of secularism.
Thus, Catholic anti-Communism was, at its core, opposition to secularism.
Catholics called for a reassertion of traditional values, particularly in the
realms of science and of the family. Secularism, they argued, had upended
gender relations and had privileged scientific belief over religion.

Many Marian devotees criticized the view that man could understand the universe solely through scientific methods. Schorn warned, "Misapplied science has so puffed men up that they loudly proclaim their self-sufficiency, and are even denying, in increasing numbers, the very existence of a Supreme Being."[41] One member of a Detroit block Rosary group who shared Schorn's critique wrote that "science, armaments, manpower have their definite value in our national life, but it is America on its knees which will turn the hand of the Almighty in our behalf to bring about a just and lasting peace for the entire world."[42] These Catholics did not reject science; however, they questioned the assumed supremacy of scientific expertise that was so prevalent during the postwar period. They insisted that the traditional absolute values expressed by the Church had to be reinfused into American culture.[43]

Many Marian devotees focused particularly on the patriarchal family, which they believed was threatened by secular American culture. As a result of both the Great Depression and World War II, numerous married women held jobs.[44] Catholic newspapers and public speakers during the period immediately after World War II repeatedly warned that the nation would come to a crashing halt if traditional gender roles were not reasserted. John J. Maher, the Michigan Commander of the Catholic War Veterans, argued that the home, the cradle of "democracy, religion, industry, discipline, and moral and civil training," had to be maintained if American civilization were to survive.[45] Father Patrick Peyton worried that secularist Americans had abandoned traditional sources of moral authority, thus weakening American society and making it susceptible to the lure of "totalitarian slavery." According to Peyton, the main battleground was the family, which Peyton believed was in "very grave danger." As evidence of this malaise, Peyton pointed to the rise in juvenile delinquency and postulated that crime and immorality would continue to increase if the family were not strengthened. He stated that if we "let the family disappear . . . civilization will disappear; or the life that will be left will not be livable or human."[46]

In response to this family crisis, Maher and Peyton turned to a model that a number of Catholics adopted: Mary. As Maher said, "All down through the ages, She [the Church] has laid down for mankind, a perfect formula for a perfect home. She gave us the perfect home, established and maintained by St. Joseph and the Virgin Mary, that carried religion, industry, simplicity and discipline, and all the other things that are conducive of good."[47] Father Peyton encouraged Catholics to embrace Mary through the Family Rosary Crusade, a radio program Peyton founded in which families gathered together around the radio to pray for the conversion of

Russia and world peace.[48] He encapsulated the idea behind the devotion
in the famous motto of the Family Rosary Crusade: "The family that prays
together stays together."[49]

Like many other Americans, Marian devotees sought to reinvent the "traditional" family during the postwar era by urging women to leave their jobs
and center their lives on their homes. As Elaine Tyler May has noted, "The
legendary family of the 1950s . . . represented something new. It was not,
as common wisdom tells us, the last gasp of 'traditional' family life with
roots deep in the past."[50] Catholic fears of secularism led devotionalists to
assert their beliefs in the public sphere in order to reshape the family along
patriarchal lines.

Marianists strove to make the job of wife and mother seem more appealing to women by elevating its status even as they denied women's equality.
They celebrated Mary as the paragon of the Catholic housewife and mother.
As one *Michigan Catholic* article stated, "Modern women will not follow
the pattern of the Blessed Mother if they disdain the obscurity of the home,
or if they resent being subordinate to the husband and father whom God
has appointed head of the family."[51] Merely staying at home and caring for
their husbands and children was not enough for the good Catholic woman,
however. Marian devotees also urged her to emulate the qualities that made
Mary the ideal woman. In a prayer for the consecration of mothers to Mary,
for example, mothers pledged to "lead a life like that of yours. Your care for
the Christ Child will teach me to watch over my children; your solicitude
for St. Joseph will guide me in love for my husband; your patience, charity
and humility will show me how to live in peace with my neighbors. . . . My
aim will be to be a 'Mother like unto Mary'; your life will be my inspiration;
your name will be my watchword."[52] Catholic women were encouraged to
embrace their subordinate role. As Cardinal Mooney of Detroit pointed
out, "When God's will was made clear to her in the supreme crisis of her
life, [Mary] bowed her head in all simplicity and humility and said 'Behold
the handmaid of the Lord, be it done to me according to Thy Word.'"[53]

Although the Church hierarchy pushed this conservative restructuring of
gender roles onto Catholic women, their Marian rhetoric proved popular
among Catholic laywomen. In the St. Rose of Lima Parish on the east side of
Detroit, for instance, more than forty block Rosary groups began during the
Korean war as part of the parish's crusade for peace.[54] The parish newsletter
exalted Mary's role as the Mother that all Catholics could go to with their
problems. "No mother was ever more anxious to help her children than
Mary is to help us," the *St. Rose Messenger* stated. "Talk to her through
the Rosary." The newsletter likened American mothers' situation with that

of Mary, since Mary too had a "Son in Service." Like a soldier in the army, Christ "gave His life for His fellowmen. So Mary really understands the anguish of a mother's heart."[55] Many Catholic women eagerly embraced the Marian ideal, even though they recognized that not all women could afford to be full-time, stay-at-home mothers. As the women's editor of the *Michigan Catholic* put it, "It is especially important that women honor Mary in a world which belittles everything she stands for. Our secularistic and materialistic society considers it demeaning to perform those household tasks which she spiritualized by her attitude towards them." The editor argued, as did other Marian devotees, "If there were more women like Mary, there would be more men like Christ."[56]

A majority of Catholic women in Detroit said that they agreed with this celebration of domesticity. In a survey of Detroit residents done in 1956, nonworking women were asked to describe the things that made them feel most useful. Catholic women were far more likely than their Protestant counterparts to answer that homemaking and childrearing gave them the greatest sense of accomplishment.[57] Likewise, among women who worked outside of the home, non-Catholics were more likely to say that working or having a regular job gave them the greatest sense of satisfaction than were Catholics.[58] Thus, Catholic women embraced the fight against secular values and perceived their roles as wives and mothers in hierarchical, patriarchal families as a status that gave their lives' meaning. The Catholic fight against secularism proved very successful as many Americans embraced what had long been the ideal Catholic model of the family.

Building Community

Many Catholics also worried that the culture of the Detroit area had become highly secular. The Detroit area in the 1940s and 1950s had the characteristics of a boomtown—massive influx of people, rapid turnover in some neighborhoods, and tension between long-time and newer residents.[59] In addition, thousands of white Detroiters left the city for the suburbs during these decades. As a result, the public sphere was in flux. Different groups—labor unions, African Americans, small businessmen, Communist Party members, churchgoers—all fought to control the public discourse and assert their ideas. Catholics proclaimed their cultural values in this rapidly changing community by building churches in new suburbs and by sharing Rosary devotions with their neighbors.

Catholics in these new communities faced far different problems than those they had confronted in the prewar city. On the one hand, Detroit residents were moving out of the ethnic enclaves into areas that lacked the tight Catholic subcultures of the old neighborhoods.[60] This created a problem for the American church, since Catholicism stresses the communitarian nature of society. Traditional Catholic values emphasize the network of social connections in which each person exists. In the new suburban communities, these social connections could be disrupted. Catholics in the suburbs were far more likely to live in close proximity with non-Catholics and their supposedly secular, materialistic values. Many Catholic commentators worried that, as Catholics moved into neighborhoods and worked in corporations next to Protestants, Catholics would seek to fit in by no longer attending mass. In addition, postwar affluence created a crisis for Catholics since materialism and consumerism potentially weakened spirituality and piety. In reaction to these two related threats, the hierarchy and the laity helped create a new Catholic community in the suburbs.[61] The most tangible manifestations of this community building were the eighty-two new parishes the Detroit archdiocese built between 1945 and 1958.[62] The *Michigan Catholic* continually urged classified-ad readers to "Look here for homes in Catholic parishes" and regularly published articles and photo spreads of the new suburban churches and schools. Developers often included the names of the new churches in their ads for suburban communities in hopes that Catholics would be more likely to move into areas with established parishes.

The hierarchy and the laity jointly formed devotional cultures in these new communities. The archdiocese recognized that "if our Catholic people remain disunited in their sacrificial actions, they will probably also remain disunited and ineffectual in their thinking, their planning and in their influence upon their community."[63] The Americanized descendants of immigrant Catholics participated in creating this new Catholic culture by flocking to church in even greater numbers than their ancestors had. According to the Detroit Area Study, only 58 percent of first-generation Catholic immigrants reported attending church every week while 79 percent of second-generation Catholics and 85 percent of third-generation or beyond went to mass weekly.[64] These Americanized Catholics also participated in a variety of devotions, and they used these devotions to critique and reshape American culture. As Robert Orsi has pointed out, second- and third-generation Catholics readily adopted devotions during the 1940s and 1950s that helped them negotiate "a relationship with the values and procedures of the modern world . . . in which they had no choice but to live."[65] Like the followers of St. Jude, whom Orsi studied, lay participants embraced Marian devotions to help them in their struggle to make sense of rapidly changing world around them.

Yet, even as Detroit residents practiced the devotional Catholicism that had been so central to the nineteenth-century immigrant experience, they fundamentally changed its character. For immigrants during the nineteenth century, devotionalism had functioned as a system of ritual observances that both strengthened ethnic identity and set Catholics apart from their non-Catholic neighbors. Italians in Harlem venerated the statue of the Virgin that they had brought with them from the old country, Mexicans in Chicago prayed to Our Lady of Guadalupe, and Poles in Pittsburgh prayed Rosaries to the Black Madonna.[66] The block Rosary and family Rosary, at least according to its advocates, had exactly the opposite effect. Fatima devotions were not confined to any immigrant group or particular immigrant church. Fatima devotees created a new, pan-Catholic, anti-Communist veneration in their recently settled suburbs or outer-city neighborhoods. In addition, Fatima devotions did not necessarily separate Catholics from their Protestant neighbors. According to Nicholas Schorn, the block Rosary had such appeal that even Protestants participated. Implicit in Schorn's writings is the message that the Rosary's power and beauty made Protestants want to assimilate with Catholics rather than vice versa. While it is impossible to confirm Schorn's assertions, his statements nevertheless point out that Cold War–era devotionalists saw themselves as helping Catholics influence the public sphere. Their devotions did not separate different ethnic groups or Catholics from their non-Catholic neighbors. Instead, praying the Rosary for the conversion of Russia brought Catholics of every ethnicity together while simultaneously allowing them to shape the neighborhood culture along Catholic lines.[67]

Conclusion

The Catholic battle against Communism was inextricably linked to long-standing fears that secularism was undermining traditional sources of moral authority. In response, many Catholics in Detroit reasserted a particular vision of society. By drawing together the neighbors on their block or the members of their family in prayer, they used Marian devotions to express their fear of a moral crisis brought on by the modern world's rejection of supposed timeless values. However, as the history of such devotions make clear, these emerging rituals responded to contemporary cultural and political problems. Catholic anti-Communist rhetoric received a warmer response once church sympathies came in line with American cold-war policies. By defending the principles of the Atlantic Charter, Catholic anti-Communists situated themselves as the true defenders of Americanism.

Catholics during the postwar period built upon the critiques of modern society that Popes Leo XIII and Pius XI articulated in their encyclicals. Organizations like ACTU set out to defeat communism and improve conditions for industrial workers. Conservative Catholics, on the other hand, increasingly viewed Communism and secularism as far greater threats than those posed by industrial capitalism. They rejected or ignored the earlier critique of capitalism that the encyclicals included. By the late 1940s, conservative Catholics often criticized labor priests like Fr. George Higgins, who had a syndicated column in the *Michigan Catholic*, for his seeming sympathy to the "Communist" CIO.

Detroit Catholics, like other urban Northerners, were both the backbone and the bane of New Deal liberalism. During the mid-twentieth century, many of these urbanites remained loyal Democrats while simultaneously constraining liberal reform, which they often associated with Communism. Other Catholics, however, became increasingly critical of the Democrats' supposed weakness on Communism. They helped create a conservative movement during the 1950s and 1960s that embraced anti-Communism and the belief that the nation had to return to timeless, absolute values in order to defeat this perceived evil. Anticommunism was a crucial reason that some Catholics began turning against the New Deal order that they had so eagerly embraced during the 1930s and 1940s, and it is impossible to understand conservatism without exploring the grassroots culture of postwar Catholicism.[68]

CHAPTER FIVE

BUSINESS, ANTI-COMMUNISM, AND THE WELFARE STATE, 1945–1958

In January 1943 a group of top General Motors executives gathered together to discuss the corporation's plans for the postwar period. Flush with their wartime profits and power, these businessmen might have been expected to gloat in victory. Big business, after all, flourished during the war, averaging a net income during the three years of war production of $22 billion before taxes. As a result of the conflict, General Motors was in "wonderful financial shape."[1] The public's opinion of business, which had been battered during the depression, was rising at the same time as the American "miracle of production" was proving decisive in battling the Axis powers.

However, these architects of the "arsenal of democracy" were surprisingly worried about the future. Donaldson Brown, the vice chairman of GM, warned his fellow members of this Post-war Planning Group that "what we think of as private capitalism and free enterprise are threatened." This threat came, not from German Fascism or Soviet Communism, but from the American government. Brown argued that, after the war, "under the pressures which will exist it is to be feared that we may come under the blanket of a 'planned economy,' and subject to the theories of collectivism in some form or other." Brown, like many of his contemporaries in Detroit industry, perceived that the postwar period would see a battle between advocates of a planned economy and businessmen who sought to recapture the "right to manage."[2]

When Brown portrayed the battle as a stark fight between free enterprise and government planning, he exaggerated the radical nature of the opposition. The 1930s-style government planning fell out of favor during the war among many liberals, who were horrified at the actions of centralized states such as Germany and Japan. By the 1940s, few New Dealers advocated a planned economy that would redistribute wealth. Instead, liberals increasingly sought to create a high-wage, low-price economy that would encourage mass consumption.[3]

However, businessmen were disturbed by the government's intervention during both the New Deal and the war, and they worried that liberal policy-makers would want to continue wartime economic controls after the fighting ended. Executives during the final years of World War II and the early years of the Cold War peppered their writings and speeches with diatribes against collectivism, planned economies, and Communism.[4] Surprisingly, however, they spent little time discussing the Kremlin or the American Communist Party when they warned against the collectivist threat. For most Detroit businessmen, the face of collectivism was UAW President Walter Reuther or Governor G. Mennan Williams, not Josef Stalin. Nor was their perceived sense of threat exaggerated. Business leaders argued that the liberal left sought to increase the power and scope of the state, which it did. Corporate managers discussed such issues as social security, unemployment insurance, and peacetime price controls, all measures that most executives saw as part of the "march toward socialism or collectivism" and that labor-liberals believed were key to creating a modern welfare state.[5]

Many Detroit business leaders believed that the New Deal state endangered free enterprise. While they were certainly anti-Communist, they talked far more about the threat posed by the welfare state than they did about the Soviet Union. These men made little distinction between the New Deal, Socialism, and Communism. The former, they argued, would ultimately lead to the latter. As a result, Detroit business leaders during the late 1940s and 1950s carried out a campaign to check state power. Like other American businessmen, they believed that they had to sell free enterprise in order to stop the welfare state and ultimately defeat Socialism and Communism. Their libertarian critique of the welfare state became a central component of modern conservatism.[6]

World War II and Planning

The battle to shape the postwar political economy began during WWII and arose in response to the increasing power of both organized labor (as discussed in chapter 1) and the federal government. The Roosevelt administration used its authority to organize the economy to defeat the Axis powers. Federal agencies such as the Office of Price Administration (OPA) set wage guidelines, implemented price controls, and rationed gasoline, rubber, and meat, while the War Production Board (WPB) created production quotas and built new factories throughout the country.[7]

The growth in both labor and state power increased business's hostility to the New Deal state and to newly empowered unions. As table 1 in chapter 2 pointed out, executives, professionals, owners of small businesses, and white-collar workers in particular criticized labor and the federal government for having too much power and for imposing burdensome regulations. One businessman complained, "After you work hard all day, you hate all that paper work. It's a pain in the neck." Another worried that such regulations might threaten freedom: "We are a free people, and we want to stay that way. Of course, we are not so free any more. Our regulations and restrictions are getting worse and worse." A powerful government, in conjunction with the enormous wartime deficit that was being created, could even end private enterprise after the war: "We will be so deep in debt that we will have to have a change. A lot of us feel we are going more Socialistic. There will be less millionaires and less income."[8]

Corporate public relations campaigns thus found an increasingly sympathetic audience during the last years of the war. General Motors was in the forefront of fight against state expansion and union power. In a 1943 meeting of the General Motors Post-war Planning Policy Group, Donaldson Brown warned that "unless industry, for its own part, is ready with a 'Plan' when the war is over, then the only alternative will be for Government to do the planning." He feared that government bureaucrats were only too willing to tell corporations how many "automobiles, refrigerators, washing machines, housing projects, and so on" they should produce.[9] Corporations had to win over the American public to business ways of thinking, especially since surveys indicated that key segments of the population hoped that government would continue controlling the economy after the war.[10]

In order to prevent the creation of such a planned economy after the war, management argued that private initiative had been responsible for the successful wartime mobilization. Their logic resembled that of German and Italian businessmen who had used the historical legacy of bourgeois liberalism and laissez-faire capitalism's failure before and during World War I as a rationale for the creation of a powerful centralized government during the 1930s. American executives pointed to the success of liberal capitalism during World War II to justify the return to a less regimented, less centralized state.[11] General Motors President Charles E. Wilson testified to the Congressional Special Committee on Post-war Economic Policy and Planning that mass production had been the "real secret weapon of our country." Without such production, "no matter how brave and experienced our fighting men are, without the right weapons this modern mechanized war could not be won." This industrial production, General Motors pointed out in its 1945 annual report, had not occurred miraculously. In fact, industry's contribution "was inherent in the social and economic way of life which had grown up in America over a long period of years—a way of life which encouraged individual initiative and developed skills and abilities readily adaptable to fighting and producing for victory." Industry had produced technologically superior weapons in a short time because of "the constant pressure of commercial competition," not because of government planning. Individual initiative and competitive capitalism, according to GM executives, led to the Allied production victory.[12]

General Motors Strike

As soon as the war ended, GM sought to turn back the New Deal by weakening labor and ending federal wage and price controls. GM executives realized that they would have to defeat the UAW, one of the most powerful liberal institutions in the country, to achieve their goals. Both General Motors and the United Auto Workers recognized that the battle to shape the postwar economy would begin as soon as conversion from wartime to peacetime production started. The UAW advocated the creation of a system in which labor and government, along with management, would shape wage, price, and profit policy to ultimately create a high-wage, low-price economy that could sustain mass consumption. The first confrontation between GM and the UAW—the 1945–46 GM strike—thus took on much greater import in this environment. The walkout began after the UAW urged the Truman administration to maintain its wartime price control policies, even after wage controls were relaxed. Union leaders argued that GM could afford a 30 percent wage hike without a subsequent increase in auto prices. When GM denied that it could raise wages without boosting prices, Walter Reuther called for GM to open its books to allow labor and consumers to see GM's financial state.

GM's management shared the UAW's goal of creating a high-wage, high-consumption economy. However, they rejected government intervention as the best means to encourage mass consumption, and they criticized any businesses that acquiesced to government price controls. GM chairman Alfred Sloan particularly objected to U.S. Steel's 1945 agreement that it would increase wages if the OPA would allow the company to raise prices. Sloan's refusal to support controls became GM's policy during the strike that began in November 1945.[13] GM criticized the Truman administration for its "unsound" economic policies, which relaxed wage controls while still regulating prices, and management blamed these actions for the labor unrest. "[I]f prices are to be regulated by the Government," GM claimed, "wages must also be regulated. The economy cannot be partly regimented and partly free." GM executives welcomed the strike as a way to rid business of the remaining and much-hated governmental wartime regulations. They condemned Reuther's call to open the books as a "direct invasion of managerial responsibility" and characterized his plan to raise wages while holding prices steady with government price controls "an economic absurdity." While GM's management agreed that "labor has the right to organize for the purposes of bargaining collectively" in order to increase wages, they sought to weaken government's role in labor-management relations.[14]

General Motors and its business allies embarked on a public-relations campaign to defeat the union and reorient popular support from labor-liberalism to business values. GM even published a cartoon version of economist Friedrich Hayek's enormously popular 1944 book, *The Road to Serfdom*, which ran in *Life* magazine in 1945. In a mere eighteen panels, the cartoon explained Hayek's libertarian argument. According to this popularization of Hayek, "Wartime 'planners' who want to stay in power" would encourage the idea of a "peace production board." The planners would control the press to educate people about their ideas. As the planners failed to implement their scheme, the public would clamor for a leader who could make the plan work. Ultimately, a "strong man" would be given power. The centralized economy established by this new totalitarian government would be "clumsy, unfair, [and] inefficient." GM thus used Hayek's argument to explain what conservatives saw as the dangers of the UAW's tripartite strategy to control prices, wages, and profits. Planning, according to Hayek, would eventually destroy constitutional liberties, the democratic process, and capitalism. The quality of life for all citizens would decrease as the inefficient economy proved unable to provide the goods that Americans wanted. General Motors, on the other hand, argued that they acted for the betterment of the public. The harmony of interests between business and the public was so complete, according to Donaldson Brown, that GM commonly used the saying "What is good for the country is good for General Motors." While management portrayed labor as acting only in its narrow self-interest, businessmen argued that they recognized their larger social responsibility of protecting the American economy.[15]

Despite GM's best efforts, the majority of Americans in December 1945 supported labor's call that General Motors workers receive pay increases to compensate for the end of overtime.[16] As the wife of one GM worker stated, "I've got my man and four kids to feed. We can't do it if we have to take a cut in pay, and that's what the forty-hour week means, unless they give us more per hour. It's just as simple as that. I'm behind my man."[17] In response, auto executives from other corporations threw their support behind GM's propaganda efforts. They echoed Wilson's condemnation of Reuther's ideas as dangerously inflationary, a powerful criticism in the overheated economy of the postwar period. They contended that the UAW's plan would not increase workers' standards of living but would instead erode their purchasing power. High wages, business leaders claimed, came from business investment, not from labor's political program. Henry Ford II insisted that "higher wages can come only out of greater production and lower cost" if inflation was to be avoided. He pointed out that union leaders "enjoy a social power of enormous proportions" and implicitly blamed labor bosses for shortages in consumer goods by arguing that "if they are going to be real leaders, they must accept the social obligations that go with leadership."[18] George Romney warned that, until the nation rejected the "scarcity-breeding idea that purchasing power is increased by hiking wage rates without regard to production results, will we stop the inflationary spiral that Walter Reuther and his economic followers set in motion."[19] In their quest to reorient workers' loyalty away from labor and the expansive New Deal state, executives credited business with providing American workers with a high standard of living and blamed labor for inflation, scarcity, and unemployment.

GM succeeded in its drive to limit the scope of labor's collective bargaining power and win public support for its position. Although Reuther ultimately won an 18.5-cent-per-hour pay hike, management was the true victor in the lengthy strike that ended in March 1946. The corporation stood fast in its determination to pay only the "going rate" for labor and rejected the UAW's demand that unions and government have a say in setting prices and wages. General Motors used the raise as a justification for a price increase, and labor's wage boosts were rapidly consumed by inflation. Most important, management turned back the UAW's challenge to its managerial prerogatives and rejected greater government interference in its labor relations. By November 1946, as consumer support for price controls dropped precipitously, the Truman administration lifted price restrictions and ultimately pulled the plug on the Office of Price Administration (OPA). In the war to shape the postwar state, General Motors and its business allies triumphed in the first major battle.[20]

Selling Free Enterprise:
The Fight against Monopoly Unionism

The Republicans' resounding victories in the 1946 congressional elections appeared to further confirm that business successfully convinced the public to reject the labor-liberal agenda. With a Republican majority in Congress, the business community seized its chance to weaken organized labor, the most powerful advocate for the expansion of the welfare state. The National Association of Manufacturers (NAM) led the fight to amend the Wagner Act, the basis of labor's strength.

This lobbying effort marked a changing of the guard within the organized business community. During the New Deal and World War II, more moderate business organizations like the Chamber of Commerce of the United States (CCUS), the Business Advisory Council (BAC), and the Committee on Economic Development (CED) were the foremost business advocacy groups. These associations had accommodated organized labor and the New Deal. The NAM, on the other hand, had been a largely ineffectual organization during Roosevelt's presidency. The public saw it as too conservative, even reactionary, since the association regularly called for the Wagner Act's repeal and the New Deal's dismantling. However, during World War II, NAM restructured its staff and board in order to increase its effectiveness. While NAM's goals did not substantively change, its rhetorical emphasis did. Rather than calling for the obliteration of the still-popular New Deal, NAM increasingly argued that labor law needed to be reformed to protect the public from labor's power.[21] The NAM's Industrial Relations Policy Committee adopted a program that called for revision of the Wagner Act to make it "fair" and for limitations on the right to strike against the "public interest." It packaged this agenda in a way that sought to "place the onus of industrial discord on unions for refusing to accept reasonable reforms to protect the public." By 1946, the once-marginalized NAM had successfully recaptured the mantle of business leadership from the more moderate Chamber of Commerce of the United States (CCUS).[22]

The NAM's new strategy became the basis for the labor legislation it backed in 1947. In the public-relations campaign to support this labor law reform, advocates of this legislation complained that the Wagner Act had given labor "monopoly power." The proposed amendment to the Wagner Act restricted union strength by banning closed-shop contracts and secondary boycotts, denying access to the National Labor Relations Board (NLRB) for Communist-led unions, eliminating unionization among foreman, and ending industry-wide collective bargaining. Business leaders justified these restrictions on labor by arguing that unchecked union dominance would ultimately harm the public interest. Charles E. Wilson of GM claimed that, if competing employers were forced to "deal on an industry wide basis with industry-wide monopolistic unions, employer cartels to match them are thereby made inevitable." "In the end," Wilson warned, "the State will have to step in and control both to protect the interests of all the people." Industrialists would thus feel compelled to create cartels in order to compete with powerful unions. The government would have to intervene and take a larger role in managing the economy. Once again, business portrayed its actions as protecting the public interest even as it weakened organizations that safeguarded workers.[23]

Wilson encouraged Americans to observe the situation in England as a lesson in the pitfalls of expanded state power and "socialistic experiments." Because the English economy under the Labour Party was inherently inefficient, Wilson asserted, the government would eventually need to impose economic controls in order to meet production goals. While state control over the economy might lead to increased output, such governmental control threatened constitutional liberties. Wilson questioned "whether England can achieve efficient production in its socialized industries without resorting to coercion and the destruction of essential personal freedoms and, finally, the dictatorship which has been the result of such political philosophy in all other countries."[24] An editorial in the New York Times echoed Wilson's logic and spelled out its implications. "What Mr. Wilson perceives clearly," the unnamed Times editor stated, "is that unless the Government is prepared to be constantly on guard against the rise of monopoly in any and every quarter, whether in the field of industry or labor, the country will have no conscious choice in the matter. For it is precisely this process of cartelization," the editor argued, "that leads sooner or later to socialization, and, through socialization, all too often the rest of the way to complete totalitarianism."[25] Only a free market economy, business advocates argued, would protect basic constitutional rights. They asserted that the welfare state which organized labor sought would inevitably lead the nation down the slippery slope to Socialism and Soviet-style totalitarianism.[26]

This equation of labor's monopoly power with totalitarianism highlighted a key element of business's logic. While the restrictions on Communists in unions became the most famous element of NAM's proposed legislation, the Communist Party was not the main target of the law.[27] Although the businessmen who advocated reform of labor legislation were staunch anti-Communists, they recognized that American capitalism faced little threat from the American Communist Party. As one author argued in the *Bulletin of the Small Business Men's Association*, "The real communists are not in Hollywood. Nor are they to be found in any substantial number in the rank and file of American labor unions." Instead, he claimed, "The real collectivists and socialists are in Washington—in the high places of government, in the high councils of national labor unions, in the high councils of the Democratic party." The leftists that Americans needed to combat were not those in league with a foreign government, especially since "America has only a handful of communists who sympathize with totalitarianism in Russia or are really working in the interests of a foreign power." The true threat came from loyal Americans who were the "enemies of our risk-capital system." These people were dangerous because they had a "sincere conviction that state socialism is better for America than the 'free enterprise system.'" They were good liberals who "really want government capital and government control substituted and some form of planned economy established, with the government as master." Liberal advocates of government planning and their labor allies, not American Communists, were the true targets of the business campaign against the Wagner Act.[28]

The business community achieved a limited but important victory when Congress passed almost all of its key demands in the Taft-Hartley Act. The only NAM plank that Congress failed to pass was the prohibition on industry-wide bargaining, and this remained a key issue for business throughout the 1950s.

Mobilizing Business

The Republicans' success at checking labor and government power with the Taft-Hartley Act made their failure in the 1948 election a tremendous surprise. Just when it appeared that business leaders and their allies were winning the public-relations battle against labor-liberals, Harry Truman recaptured the presidency with a platform that called for extending the New Deal. In Congress, a new generation of liberal activists took office, while in Michigan the liberal G. Mennan Williams won the governor's race. In the ongoing battle between conservatives and liberals to shape the postwar state, Michigan liberals appeared to win a crucial victory.

The Republican defeat was an especially bitter setback for Detroit businessmen because the CIO in 1948 had "captured" the Michigan Democrats with the objective of remolding the party "into a real liberal and progressive political party which can be subscribed to by members of the CIO and other liberals." The UAW in particular encouraged its members to work on the precinct, ward, county, and congressional level to get out the vote and elect candidates who supported prolabor, prowelfare state policies. The Michigan CIO's Political Action Committee (PAC) was instrumental in Williams's successful campaign over incumbent Republican Kim Sigler.[29]

The 1948 defeat convinced Detroit businessmen that they needed to redouble their efforts to check government expansion. The Detroit Board of Commerce led the call to arms. Board member Julian McIntosh criticized businessmen who "have developed a belief that politics is beneath us, that it is a sordid business." He warned his fellow board members that they faced increasing numbers of "proposals coming from Washington designed to regiment the people and our economy" that would lead "directly to State Socialism."[30] Other Detroit businessmen urged their peers to do a better job at convincing Americans of the superiority of free enterprise. Herbert R. Dusendorf of the Nelson Company of Detroit, complained that the "country has been drifting with constantly increasing speed toward some sort of collectivism, toward a government controlled economy" in response to the demands of the American people. Dusendorf urged business leaders to change the American people's wants. Businessmen had only themselves to blame for not selling free enterprise more actively. He pointed to some key welfare-state policies, like social security, unemployment insurance, peacetime price controls, rent controls, "or any of the other measures which have constituted another stride in the march toward socialism or collectivism" and questioned whether his fellow businessmen had tried to stop their adoption. "If you have not consciously done something to help preserve the American System," Dusendorf chided, "then you may be sure that you have unconsciously done something to aid in tearing it down."[31] If Detroit businessmen did not mobilize, the resurgent Democrats could wipe out the gains business had made since the war and could further expand the New Deal state.

Fighting the Garrison State

As American interests expanded to include territories overseas during the early twentieth century, the federal government grew in scope and power. The domestic impact of this growth was minimal until U.S. security was threatened in World War II and the Cold War. In response, the Roosevelt, Truman, and Eisenhower administrations, in conjunction with the military, strengthened the federal government, particularly the executive branch. They increased federal spending, called for higher taxes, and created or expanded large new bureaucracies like the Pentagon, the Central Intelligence Agency (CIA), and the National Security Council (NSC). In addition, some governmental strategists argued that the nation could no longer fight wars if industrial planning was left in the hands of the private sector. The United States, these policymakers argued, needed a strong central government bureau that would direct industrial production in order to ensure that private needs were not subordinated to military demands.[32]

Powerful opposition groups sought to check or shape this state expansion. The New Deal and the planning of WWII had mobilized these antistatists, and they vowed to defend the practice of weak, decentralized government. Many antistatists shared the view expressed by Friedrich Hayek in *The Road to Serfdom*—"planning leads to dictatorship."[33] They feared that the next conflict would be a total war that could only be won with a complete national commitment to the fight. In such a war, they warned, every aspect of American life would come under governmental control. As conservative congressman Wat Arnold warned during the Marshall Plan debate, expanded American global commitments might ultimately create "a police state at home."[34] Political scientists like Harold Lasswell called this the garrison state. Under such a regime, the government would maintain domestic order by suspending constitutional liberties while managing the economy in order to maximize military viability. Opponents of state power viewed such a possibility with horror.[35]

Businessmen were in the forefront of the opposition to government industrial planning and the creation of a garrison state, particularly once the Korean War began. They complained bitterly as the Truman administration pushed a package of wage-and-price controls and tax increases through Congress.[36] Corporate leaders also grumbled as the administration responded to CIO demands that labor play a larger role in managing the war economy in hopes of reestablishing the tripartite system that had existed during World War II. Organized labor was indeed given a seat on the Wage Stabilization Board (WSB) in response to CIO pressures.[37]

Despite their aspirations, labor leaders quickly found themselves disappointed in the administration's actions. The regulations the federal government adopted in January 1951 appeared to favor business. The WSB was quickly subsumed by the Office of Defense Mobilization, which was controlled by Charles E. Wilson of General Electric. The Truman administration established price ceilings on a cost-plus basis, which allowed industry to pass on higher costs to the consumer. Rather than adopting strict price controls in order to limit inflation, the government relied on the Federal Reserve, which restricted credit to suppress consumer demand.[38] As inflation rose, workers struck for higher wages. Labor leaders pressured Truman to adopt stringent price guidelines and more flexible wage stabilization policies rather than wage freezes. However, when the Wage Stabilization Board passed a wage freeze on February 15, 1951, furious CIO leaders resigned from the WSB in protest.[39]

Nevertheless, industrialists chafed at federal controls because they interpreted even the weak wage-and-price regulations as a back-door attempt to create a planned economy. The combination of tax raises, economic controls, and labor's demand for an expanded voice in the economy mobilized business groups to block any additional governmental expansion. Charles E. Wilson of General Motors (not to be confused with "Electric" Charles Wilson of GE) warned that "since the desire and ability to buy are denied in the marketplace and government controls decide who gets what and how much he should pay, economic freedom is lost and with it many of our other freedoms." Wilson even went so far as to state that "many are coming to believe that the immediate danger of a third world war is lessening; many more believe that the danger of losing our free society through our own internal policies is increasing."[40] Wilson interpreted the government's acceptance of relatively weak controls to fight inflation as the opening wedge in the administration's attempt to regulate the entire economy and ultimately create the garrison state. Even in the midst of the Korean War, the greater threat to the nation came from within, according to Wilson.

Other Detroit industry leaders echoed Wilson's complaints about controls. L. L. Colbert, president of Chrysler, grumbled that the government decided how much steel, copper and aluminum would be allocated for building cars and trucks and then informed each auto company of exactly how many vehicles it could build. Ernest Breech of Ford claimed that domestic liberty was threatened by bureaucrats who sought to substitute "some form of centralized, omniscient planning for the normal pattern of our free economy." Breech likened these government controls to those adopted by the Soviet Union and the British. "[W]hen we say the Soviet system has failed or that British socialism has come near to destroying the economy of Britain, what we mean is that planning has failed—because it is impossible for controls and the free, independent spirit of humanity to exist together in the same national community." For both Colbert and Breech, Korean mobilization was leading to just the sort of planned economy that businessmen had feared in 1945 and 1946. Even though the controls were temporary and relatively pro-business, once planning was introduced it might well become an accepted governmental role. Detroit manufacturers complained that if government continued to set price ceilings and allocate materials, the nation would begin the slippery slide toward the garrison state and would ultimately adopt Soviet-style totalitarianism.[41]

Detroit manufacturers also had a very tangible reason to protest against federal mobilization efforts—these policies sent the Detroit economy into a sharp recession in late 1951 and early 1952. Production for the civilian market fell during the third quarter of 1951 as the government restricted passenger car production in order to make steel available for defense contractors. However, defense work didn't replace passenger car production because the Office of Defense Mobilization adopted a policy of not placing large amounts of defense work in areas of concentrated manufacturing like Detroit. One year after the Korean War began, only 11 percent of Detroit's industrial workforce was employed in defense work. Auto manufacturers were major suppliers of munitions, but most of this production occurred outside of Detroit.[42] As a result, small Detroit businesses that subcontracted with the major auto companies were hit particularly hard.[43] Small machine and tool-and-die manufacturers complained that they could not procure enough steel, and what little steel was available was being sold to large corporations or being sent to munitions manufacturers outside of Detroit. Without the necessary materials, the small machine shops could not fulfill their contracts and so were forced to lay off workers. By December 1951, unemployment in Detroit reached 8 percent. Conditions worsened to such an extent that three thousand unemployed men lined up for snow-shoveling jobs and had to be controlled by the police. While the national economy boomed, Detroit suffered. Government industrial planning thus threatened economic viability as well as constitutional liberties according to Detroit manufacturers.[44]

Deindustrialization

The Korean War mobilization sped up a process that had begun years earlier: automation in conjunction with the movement of manufacturers out of Detroit into the suburbs, the rural Midwest, or the South. When Detroit businesses began leaving the city in the late 1940s and early 1950s, some Detroit workers attempted to stop this job flight. Members of UAW Local 600 from Ford, in conjunction with the National Negro Labor Council (NNLC), criticized runaway business for depriving workers of their "inalienable right to a job." This right, they claimed, grew out of the New Deal's promise of economic security. By moving out of Detroit, the NNLC claimed, corporations particularly deprived African American workers of their right to jobs. Moving to the South, where wages were lower and factories were segregated, reinforced the southern wage scale and denied high-wage employment to southern blacks. Thus, according to the NNLC, decentralization systematically threatened the rights of both northern and southern workers. Local 600's protest against decentralization was so vocal that Ford moved some machines out of the River Rouge plant at night in order to avoid worker action. Once the local realized that strikes and protests were having little impact, they filed a lawsuit against Ford for breach of contract. Under the terms of the five-year contract the UAW and Ford had negotiated in 1950, workers "became entitled to and received certain valuable rights, including . . . the right to employment in accordance with seniority at said plant." The local insisted that corporations did not have the right to move at will without any input from workers.[45]

Detroit industrialists rejected Local 600's expansive view of worker rights, as did the court. Businessmen criticized the New Deal and its promises of economic security. Peter Hsian of the Detroit Board of Commerce complained about "expanding and expending" government that sought "more and more control over the lives and pursuits of its citizens—encroaching constantly on individual rights—all in the name of security." He asserted, "Security as thus proposed is an illusion. There is no true economic security except as one creates his own, under a system of individual freedom and opportunity."[46] Detroit executives argued that the expansive welfare state's promise of economic security threatened American constitutional liberties. Only free enterprise, they argued, could protect both the worker's economic interests and personal freedoms.[47]

In order to answer Local 600's criticism that irresponsible runaway businesses were depriving Detroiters of their right to work, local executives argued that expansive government and high taxes were driving jobs out of the city. In 1950 the Board of Commerce reported that a survey of manufacturers who had moved from Detroit found that the vast majority blamed high personal property and real estate taxes for pushing them from the city to the suburbs.[48] Seven years later, a survey done by the City Plan Commission revealed that the personal property tax was the number one reason that management considered moving outside of the city limits.[49] The board complained that no other city assessed inventories for the personal property tax as high as did Detroit.[50] This tax on business inventories became a particular target for the Detroit Board of Commerce, which complained that the city overburdened business and industry while favoring residential real estate. The city's tax system protected the New Deal's promise of the right to a decent home for all Americans, and Detroit had one of the highest percentages of owner-occupied housing in the country. Detroit businessmen called on the city council to end its policy of relying on high corporate taxes to pay for social services. Deindustrialization thus was not the result of irresponsible businessmen depriving Detroit workers of their right to work, as Local 600 asserted. Instead, the Detroit Board of Commerce claimed, industrialists wanted to remain in Detroit but were being driven out by city policies that protected homeowner's rights at the expense of industry.

While many Detroit businessmen faulted city taxes for driving businesses to the suburbs, they blamed high state taxes for pushing industries out of Michigan altogether. A 1955 Board of Commerce study compared the corporate taxes in other nearby industrial states to those in Michigan and found that the corporate tax burden in Illinois and Ohio was 11 percent and 30 percent, respectively, of corporations in Michigan.[51] Harlow Curtice, president of General Motors, stated that "the present level of business taxation in Michigan has already led us to locate plants in other states, where the taxes per General Motors job are less than one-half of the present taxes per job in Michigan."[52] When the Board of Commerce surveyed its members in 1958 to find out what projects businessmen wanted the board to pursue, 84.3 percent of those replying called for the board to work for state and local tax programs that would keep Michigan businesses competitive with those in other states.[53]

In the debate over the reasons for Michigan's deindustrialization, businessmen crafted what would become another key component of postwar conservatism—opposition to taxes. They particularly targeted the "socialistic" tax policies and programs of the Democratic state government. The Detroit Board of Commerce complained that taxes had increased by 1700 percent in the eleven years in which Governor Williams had been in office, and they called for the state legislature to curtail the "ever-increasing demands for socialistic spending by the Governor" rather than raise taxes.[54] Tyrone Gillespie of Dow Chemical Company argued, "Only when we trend toward Free Enterprise and away from the Welfare State will a dynamic free business climate, full productivity and high prosperity, return."[55] In the propaganda battle between liberals and conservatives, Detroit businessmen argued that the welfare state and its resulting high taxes deprived employees of their right to work. In the battle to determine the shape of the postwar economy, businessmen fought to dismantle New Deal regulations and lower the taxes the welfare state required. They claimed that a "dynamic business environment" developed in a low-tax, low-regulation environment. Business, rather than government, would ensure workers' prosperity, according to conservatives.

The Guaranteed Annual Wage:
"The Back Door to Complete Socialism"

In addition to blaming the local and state governments for increasing the cost of doing business and driving companies out, many industrialists faulted unions, particularly the UAW. The Detroit Board of Commerce pointed to a 1959 report, "What's Ahead for Michigan?" sponsored by the Upjohn Institute for Employment Research, which stated that "industrial managers will be less attracted, other things being equal, to an area in which union membership is high and in which unions are aggressive." In his comment on the Upjohn report, Nicholas Rini of the Board of Commerce complained, "Applied to Michigan the above observation might easily qualify as the understatement of the year. Even that much-misused man-in-the-street knows that Michigan is considered the laboratory of the UAW-CIO."[56] The state's aggressive unions pushed Detroit factory workers' wages well above the national average—only New York and Chicago ranked ahead of Detroit in industrial salaries.[57]

Not all corporations objected to the high wage levels of Detroit-area workers. During the early 1950s, General Motors adopted a strategy of providing workers with cost-of-living adjustments and pensions in order to stabilize production. At the time, GM controlled 45 percent of the domestic automobile market and earned enormous returns on its investments. As a result, GM was far more interested in ending strike-related production disruptions than it was in holding down wages. General Motors executives had checked the UAW's drive to have a say in management decision making in the 1945–46 strike. Once GM restricted the union's scope to collective bargaining, the corporation was willing to reach an accommodation with Walter Reuther. In May 1950, General Motors and the UAW signed a five-year contract that provided workers with cost-of-living adjustments (COLAs), a $125-per-month pension, and company-sponsored health insurance. The UAW pressured Ford and Chrysler to follow suit; both corporations agreed to provide generous pension plans for their unionized workforce. The Big Three further expanded the relatively generous benefit package they provided their workers by instituting the guaranteed annual wage (GAW). The GAW supplemented state unemployment insurance to provide laid-off autoworkers with a high percentage of their regular pay. In 1955, for instance, Ford agreed to pay five cents per hour into a trust fund for each worker, which an employee could draw on for up to twenty-five dollars a week if he or she were laid off. When added to public unemployment compensation, Ford's payments would allow a laid-off union member to take home up to 65 percent of his or her normal pay. By the late 1960s, Reuther had successfully negotiated for supplemental benefits up to 95 percent of regular take home pay for up to fifty-two weeks of unemployment.[58]

Business journals quickly praised GM's 1950 contract with the UAW as the "Treaty of Detroit." As Daniel Bell pointed out in *Fortune*, the treaty was a milestone in industrial relations. A major corporation accepted the current distribution of wages and profits, thus abandoning any efforts to drive down costs by lowering salaries. Unlike Ford's Five-Dollar-Day, the corporation recognized the union as the legitimate bargaining power that protected high wages. The union in turn accepted the concept that worker productivity and cost of living, rather than labor's political power, determined wages.[59]

Not everyone agreed with the treaty. Labor activists both in Detroit and around the country debated whether labor's accommodation to industry was in the best interests of workers. The five-year contract meant that union militancy gave way to bureaucratized collective bargaining. Over time, workers became increasingly unaware of the union's history, and many believed that the company rather than the union was responsible for their good wages and benefits. The leaders of Local 600, in particular, criticized the Treaty as "entrapment," especially since the union agreed to accept management's prerogative in controlling production standards, work schedules, job assignments, and automation decisions—key issues the union had sought to control during the 1930s and the war. The UAW leadership found itself in the somewhat awkward position of having to silence Local 600's militancy and crack down on strikes and walkouts in order to maintain the contract.[60]

More important, the Treaty meant that the UAW, one of the most politically progressive forces in the country, essentially abandoned the fight to expand the welfare state. Autoworkers received generous private pensions, healthcare, and supplemental unemployment insurance from their employer rather than the government and thus saw little need to expend political capital on these issues. Walter Reuther believed that pensions and healthcare would ultimately become such a financial burden to corporations that management would join "shoulder to shoulder" with labor-liberals to expand the welfare state. Unemployment insurance would become so expensive that corporations would demand that government "shoulder its proper share of the cost of unemployment and its proper share of the responsibility for preventing it." Clearly, this would not be the case.[61]

Many business leaders outside of the Big Three automakers bitterly resented GM's actions.[62] One Detroit businessman complained that, as a result of GM's cost-of-living wage policy, "There are two inflationary forces in the

U.S.—Washington and General Motors."[63] Donaldson Brown of General Motors received a number of letters and news clippings from opponents of the GAW. For instance, Earl Harding, the vice president of the National Economic Council, warned that, if the big corporations guaranteed unemployment pay, "it cannot be long before workers in small industries which cannot afford a GAW will look to government for a 'subsidy' to finance their idleness." It would be impossible for most American companies to guarantee an annual wage, Harding argued, "unless the country adopts a nationally planned economy with new government agencies to control flow of commodities, manpower, machinery, investment and financing." The GAW, according to Harding, was an "out-and-out move toward complete Socialism, and the Left-wing adherents of it are using the back door to make their way."[64] The guaranteed annual wage was the proverbial camel's nose under the tent that would lead first to government regulation of virtually every aspect of business management and ultimately, in the words of the Economic Council, to a "swift descent into either a fascist or communist dictatorship."[65]

Small businessmen found the GAW especially threatening. Thomas G. Ritter, president of Thomas A. Edison Inc., pointed out that companies with contractual obligations to pay unemployment insurance to their workers would want to keep their workers employed as much as possible. As a result, these companies "would tend to make on the premises more parts in order to fulfill those guarantees" and would shift work "from independent suppliers to the plants of the final assembler." The thousands of small machine shops and parts suppliers in Detroit could lose much of their business if the Big Three moved production into their own factories.[66] Ritter's prediction proved accurate. During the mid- and late-1950s, the Big Three curbed their reliance on independent suppliers and increasingly manufactured their own auto parts, often outside Detroit. As a result, such firms as Bohn Aluminum, Falls Spring and Wire, F. L. Jacobs, Thompson Products, Richard Brothers, and Federal Mogul closed their Detroit plants during the mid-1950s.[67]

Many labor historians and economists have argued that the Treaty of Detroit was part of a "labor-management accord" that developed after World War II and reached its height during the 1950s. According to this view, organized labor and big business made a tacit agreement: labor conflict would decrease in exchange for decent wages and benefits. Business, according to these scholars, thus accepted the legitimacy of industrial unions. More recently, historians have questioned whether this accord actually existed at the time or whether labor's supporters during the Reagan era manufactured such an accord in order to critique 1980s union bashing.[68] While it is less and less clear if this accord materialized between big business and big labor, it is quite clear that it did not exist for the owners of Detroit's small businesses. This group adamantly opposed the Treaty of Detroit and the Guaranteed Annual Wage and was instrumental in creating the nascent conservative movement that fought against them.

Harvey Campbell, the long-time executive vice president of the Detroit Board of Commerce, was an example of just such a conservative business-man. Campbell, known as "Mr. Detroit" during his forty-year tenure with the board, was a partner in the firm Apel-Campbell Advertising Designers when he became a member of the Detroit Board of Commerce in 1913. In 1940, Campbell became the executive vice president, the board's top-paid professional staff member. Of the thirty-eight hundred firms represented by the Board of Commerce in the 1950s, approximately 75 percent were small businesses.[69] Campbell was thus in tune with the grievances the owners of Detroit's small businesses felt, and he wrote about these in his weekly column in the *Detroiter*, the board's newspaper. Campbell loathed the New Deal. He complained that the welfare state undermined the work ethic in a generation of Americans by convincing "too many people . . . that the world owes them a living." The New Deal's promise of economic security, he argued, endangered American freedom since it required the growth of an ever-larger government.[70] He was especially critical of the CIO for its "socialistic policies" and its support of class divisions. "America's most dangerous menace," Campbell claimed, "is any person who makes a living creating cleavages between employer and employee."[71] He thus harkened back to an older republican view of American society, particularly to the republican emphasis on "the public good, or the good of the whole."[72] Ac-cording to republican ideology, the common good was indivisible and had to be protected from those who subverted the public good by acting out of narrow self-interest. Campbell portrayed Detroit industry as an entity that operated in the public interest by "leading the nation in initiative, invention and production." "Selfish" labor leaders, on the other hand, threatened the nation's economic vitality with their irresponsible demands. He wrote in 1957 that if unions won the war between labor and capital, there were two possible outcomes: either "Detroit labor will climb several notches higher up on Reuther's ladder leading to national socialism and workers' debase-ment, or Detroit, as a city, will add to its list of gaunt, empty factories, bereft of payrolls because of Reuther's rapacity."[73] Campbell argued that high wages and crushing taxes were part of labor's selfish program. He bitterly complained that labor was driving industry out of Detroit as it demanded ever-higher wages and as its allies in government insisted upon higher taxes. When Governor Williams called for a tax increase in 1957, for example,

Campbell warned that industrialists would no longer open factories and hire workers in Michigan. "The socialistic goose killers," Campbell claimed, have "fostered, distorted and expanded an unbalanced tax structure by telling the people that there's always more where that came from—namely job-producing industries." Reuther and Williams embodied the selfishness that Campbell believed would drive out business, destroy the city, remake the government, and hurt the workers. In 1957, an exasperated Campbell warned that "this Board of Commerce has had its fingers in the socialistic dike for a couple of generations but the rising tide is likely to swamp all of us."[74] But, by early 1958, Campbell and his fellow conservatives had found their buttress against the welfare state—Senator Barry Goldwater.

Right to Work and Goldwater

The 1957–58 recession ended the brief period of good relations between labor and the management of the Big Three. At the same time that the Eisenhower administration cut federal spending and slowed the economy, the auto industry faced its first real foreign competition as cheaper foreign cars like the Volkswagen entered the American market. Domestic auto sales plunged. The Big Three and the many companies that supplied them suddenly found that their labor costs were too high to weather the recession.[75] Not surprisingly, auto executives targeted Walter Reuther, the UAW, and Governor Williams in their drive to lower costs and weaken organized labor. Small-business owners, who had long fought Reuther and his labor-liberal allies, joined with the Big Three in this anti-labor drive.[76]

The battle against union power in Detroit was part of a nationwide conservative resurgence. Right wingers bemoaned the fact that business had gotten too cozy with labor, that the federal government had usurped powers that rightly belonged to the states, and that the Eisenhower administration had embraced "the siren song of socialism"—Keynesianism—in its fiscal year 1958 budget.[77] These conservatives criticized the "modern Republicanism" of President Eisenhower, who seemed to be forcing the Republicans to accommodate the New Deal state. The nascent conservative movement instead embraced the ideas articulated by men such as Clarence Manion, former Dean of the Notre Dame Law School and host of the weekly nationally syndicated *Manion Forum* radio program.[78] Manion had targeted unions' monopoly power and political influence from the start of his broadcast career. In one of his first shows, Manion denounced Walter Reuther for threatening every big business in the country with a strike if it did not adopt provisions similar to those in the 1955 General Motors contract. Reuther, Manion claimed, was the head of a "labor monopoly that is exempt from the antitrust law and can, therefore, callously disregard the public interest that every other person, corporation, and organization is obliged to serve."[79] Manion tirelessly worked to weaken labor's political influence by urging state legislatures to pass right-to-work legislation throughout the country. He recognized that "union shop" clauses in contracts provided labor with a steady stream of union dues, which labor leaders used to further their agenda. Right-to-work laws would diminish this stream to a trickle. Early in 1957, Manion provided ideological guidance to the successful campaign to pass this legislation in Indiana. As a result of Manion's efforts, it became illegal to dismiss employees who refused to join unions. Indiana thus became the first major industrial state to outlaw the union shop.[80]

Senator Barry Goldwater of Arizona injected many of Manion's ideas into the national political arena. He, like Manion, fought against labor's political activities. Goldwater helped popularize the conservative argument that organized labor spoke only for its leadership, not its members. These leaders, according to Goldwater, systematically abridged the free speech of the rank and file. He particularly focused on the CIO-PAC, the political organization that labor had created in the 1940s to get out the union vote and defend labor's political interests. Goldwater portrayed the PAC in the most nefarious light. Goldwater claimed, "The use of violence and coercion by union leaders has now been transferred from the area of industrial disputes and brought boldly into purely political arenas." He characterized the PAC as an un-American organization that subverted the democratic process by using union dues to push the liberal political agenda of its leadership while silencing the voices of the rank and file. To support his contention, Goldwater sponsored a press conference to give dissident union members a forum for their objections. One dissenter, a long-time member of the UAW, complained, "I bitterly oppose being compelled to make involuntary contributions through the use of my dues to finance the party which I vote against at the polls. And there are millions of rank and file men in this country who are as bitter about it as I am." The dissidents pointed to a recent study from the University of Michigan that found that more than 40 percent of union members were Republicans. To Goldwater, all of this evidence proved that labor leaders had become dictatorial as they used union dues to quash workers' voices and limit their freedom.[81]

Goldwater continued his campaign against politicized labor during the 1957 Senate Select Committee hearings that were investigating corruption in organized labor. While the rest of the committee members focused their inquires on crooked Teamsters like Jimmy Hoffa's associates "Three-Finger Brown" Lucchese, "Lefty" Rosenthal, and "Tony Ducks" Corallo, Goldwater ignored Hoffa and zeroed in on Walter Reuther, the quintessential liberal labor leader. "I would rather have Hoffa stealing my money," Goldwater asserted, "than Reuther stealing my freedom."[82] The National Association of Manufacturers agreed. On the day the Senate inquiry into improper labor activities opened, NAM released a study of "monopoly" union power that argued that Americans would be better off if the union shop were abolished. The association received support from the National Right to Work Committee, which hoped that the hearings would create a more favorable climate for legislation that would prohibit all forms of compulsory union membership. Supporters of right-to-work laws asserted that compulsory unionism destroyed individual freedom. Obligatory unionization, they claimed, subjected workers to the dictates of union autocrats and opened the door to "socialist labor dictatorship."[83] Mayor Albert Cobo of Detroit agreed. Cobo criticized Reuther for using mandatory union dues to pay for political propaganda campaigns, and he argued that Reuther was using these campaigns to try to gain control over Detroit and Michigan governments.[84]

After a few months of hearings, Goldwater managed to force the Democrats into investigating the UAW. By the end of 1957, Goldwater believed that the time was right to move against Reuther. The senator and his allies on the committee hoped to embarrass labor-liberals by publicizing UAW behavior in the long and violent strike against the Kohler Company of Wisconsin. The UAW leadership welcomed the hearing in hopes that they could counter Republican charges that the union had engaged in illegal practices against Kohler.[85]

The leaders of the Big Three and their Michigan Republican allies relished Goldwater's attack on Reuther and saw the economic downturn as a chance to finally weaken Reuther and ultimately defeat the labor-liberal alliance in Michigan. The anti-Reuther offensive heated up just as the Big Three were entering a new round of negotiations with the UAW. In mid-January, Reuther presented the union's demands for 1958. He discarded calls for a shorter work week, a strategy supported by Local 600's leaders. Cloaking himself in the mantle of loyal anti-Communism, Reuther justified this strategic change by arguing that a "combination of Russia's Sputniks and the nation's slumping economy made it necessary to forego increased leisure for the present." He instead called for a large wage increase and a profit-sharing plan for workers and customers in hopes that these proposals would stimulate the slumping economy by increasing purchasing power and production. Under Reuther's profit-sharing proposal, each auto company's net profits before taxes would be divided—50 percent to the company, 25 percent to hourly and salaried workers, and 25 percent to customers in the form of cash rebates.[86]

Leaders of the Big Three immediately joined together to express their heated opposition to the plan. Ernest Breech of Ford accused Reuther of "trying to twist and manipulate the American private-enterprise system into something more to his liking than it now evidently is." Harlow Curtice of GM stated, "This scheme is foreign to the concept of the American free enterprise system." L. L. Colbert of Chrysler claimed that Reuther's plan would be inflationary, a fact that was "not concealed from anyone by all his references to Communism, sputnik, and so forth." This attack against the UAW's bargaining position suggested to the *Detroit Free Press* that the Big Three were taking a "united front" against Reuther and that Ford in particular was departing from its usual policy of "limiting counter-attack to the bargaining table instead of taking it to the public forum."[87]

This united, public-attack strategy reached its apogee when Senator Goldwater gave the keynote address to the Wayne County Republican party at their Salute to Eisenhower dinner. GOP tacticians throughout the country were reported to be "mystified" at Goldwater's selection, since the senator had, according to the *Detroit Free Press*, "accrued something of a reputation as a reactionary in labor matters, and more especially as a determined foe of the UAW."[88] Political parties generally did not invite rabidly antilabor speakers to Detroit, particularly if they hoped to win votes in heavily unionized Wayne County. Clearly the Michigan Republicans had adopted a new adversarial strategy. Goldwater did not disappoint. The senator warned top executives from General Motors and Ford along with another thousand Republicans in attendance that "Underneath the Democrat label here in Michigan there is something new, and something dangerous—born of conspiracy and violence, sired by socialists and nurtured by the general treasury of the UAW-CIO." He told his listeners, "[I am] here tonight because I do not want to see this socialist-labor thing spread to the rest of the country, and the place to cure it, at this point, is here in Michigan." "Here in Michigan," Goldwater cautioned, "you are in the front-line trenches. We from the rest of the country are looking to you. For what happens here, can happen to the whole country." Reuther and his allies, Goldwater claimed, were "more dangerous than the Russian sputniks."[89]

The Republican Party's new willingness to take on Reuther in Michigan reportedly stemmed from its new state finance chairman, former GM vice president Don Ahrens, and was encouraged by the Board of Commerce's

Harvey Campbell. Campbell, Ahrens, and other conservatives were able to gain control of the party's agenda away from the moderate Eisenhower Republicans, who begged the party to stop their attacks on Reuther. Campbell, who was toastmaster for the dinner at the Masonic temple, said that the board had been besieged with demands that he abstain from attacking Walter Reuther. However, he vowed that he would "never stop fighting Walter Reuther. I'll never lay off." He complained that businessmen wouldn't condemn Reuther publicly because they were afraid of reprisal, but they would only "stand behind me and cheer." For the 1958 campaign, Michigan Republicans abandoned Eisenhower Republicanism and adopted the ideas of what the media referred to as the "far right wing" of the party. [90]

Michigan Republicans and their allies in the business community focused the antilabor attack on Governor Williams, who was running for reelection in 1958. The 1957–58 recession had pushed the Michigan government into a severe financial crisis, leading Williams to call on the legislature to raise taxes. Republicans howled in opposition. Governor Williams, Republican State Senator Edward Hutchinson argued, was "leading us down the road to socialism" as he spent more and more money in the state budget. High taxes to pay for Williams's social welfare policies, Republicans asserted, pushed corporations out of the state and raised local unemployment levels. Joseph Creighton, legislative representative of the Michigan Manufacturers Association, faulted "Reuther-Williams pressure for higher workmen's compensation and employment security benefits along with the guaranteed annual wage, supplemental unemployment benefits, shorter hours, higher pay and no mention of increased productivity" for the "frigid business climate" in the state. Detroit businessmen increasingly argued that the greatest threat to American capitalism came from labor-liberal attempts to expand the welfare state, not from Soviet Communism. Like Goldwater, Michigan Republicans believed that Reuther and his allies were "more dangerous than the Russian sputniks."[91]

The vicious attacks against Reuther and Williams made the Democratic victory in 1958 especially sweet to the liberal-laborites. Governor Williams retained his seat and Democrats in Congress gained their greatest victory since 1936. However, the 1958 election marked a turning point for Republicans. Goldwater was one of the few victorious Republicans, which increased his standing in the party. He became, according to one scholar, "the new conservative champion for a badly beaten GOP."[92] Michigan Republicans found that their new anti-Reuther strategy had a positive effect. A *New York Times* poll found that the party's conservative, antilabor platform "appears to be winning some recruits among independents" and was "stirring interests among orthodox Republicans."[93] Although Williams won, his margin of victory was half of what it had been in his 1956 reelection. The *Times* claimed that there was "little doubt" that the "issue of Michigan's business climate was at least partially responsible for the fall-off in the Governor's vote."[94] Even in Michigan, the bastion of labor's political strength, conservatives were building an antilabor, anti–welfare-state coalition that would lay the groundwork for the conservative ascendance of first Goldwater and later, Reagan.

Conclusion

During the 1940s and 1950s, members of the business community crafted and popularized a libertarian ideology, which became a core element of modern conservatism. They argued that the welfare state, which the New Dealers had created and which labor-liberals sought to enlarge, threatened to undermine American constitutional liberties. State intervention in the economy, they argued, would inevitably lead to totalitarianism. Free-market capitalism, on the other hand, went hand-in-hand with democracy and provided prosperity for the nation. Such a view was hardly new—Herbert Hoover had said much the same thing during the 1920s and 1930s. The Great Depression had discredited this ideology.

The wartime revival of the American economy gave business an opening to spread their ideology, and they did so vigorously. They claimed that individual initiative and unrestricted capitalism led to the Allied victory in World War II and would maintain prosperity after the war as long as government regulations did not choke the economy. High wages, they argued, came from business investment, not from labor's political program. By the end of the 1950s, conservative businessmen and their advocates, like Barry Goldwater, had created the ideological framework of modern conservatism's antistatist and antilabor strain. While earlier Republican cold warriors such as Joseph McCarthy had focused on the strategic threat presented by the American Communist Party and its Popular Front supporters among the Democrats, Goldwater and his business allies focused their critique on New Deal liberalism. They portrayed labor leaders as dictatorial and out of touch with the political views of their membership. Organized labor, they argued, drove up prices by demanding higher wages than business could afford, and their liberal allies in government raised taxes to pay for the social programs labor-liberals supported. Both actions, conservatives claimed, hurt business and, ultimately, Michigan residents as businesses fled to states with lower wages and taxes. Conservatives, on the other hand, protected free political expression and promised prosperity. In the economic downturn of the late 1950s, such rhetoric gained conservatives more adherents. Although their libertarian ideology remained marginal during the 1950s and 1960s, it became the basis for Goldwater's crucial 1964 presidential campaign. While he lost the election, the conservative ideas he popularized were central to the Republican revolution of the 1970s and 1980s.

CONCLUSION

During the 1940s, no organized conservative movement existed. Conservatives, as one scholar in the field has said, were "scattered, few in number, almost as philosophically divided as the predecessors from whom they drew inspiration."[1] Yet, as this work has shown, conservative ideas were gaining prominence in the United States. While national politics largely hewed to the principles of the New Deal during the 1940s and 1950s, local politics in Detroit was full of conservatives. There was no liberal consensus locally, particularly on issues of labor and race.

Conservatism has been the dominant political philosophy in American government for the last thirty years. Its dominance is so all-encompassing that it seems baffling to us today that scholars during the 1950s and 1960s dismissed conservatives as irrational throwbacks to a bygone era. Since the 1980s, historians have attempted to explain why and how conservatism became ascendant. Much of the early scholarship focused on the dissolution of the New Deal coalition during the late 1960s and 1970s. These scholars argued that key members of the coalition—white ethnics in the North and whites in the South—reacted to the excesses of the civil-rights movement and abandoned the Democratic Party for its continued support of black rights. More recently, historians have analyzed the development of the conservative movement rather than the dissolution of the New Deal. While some of this scholarship has looked at grassroots conservative organizations, much of it has analyzed elite conservatives, particularly key intellectuals, major politicians, and prominent business leaders.

I have argued that we can see the roots of American conservatism in the political, racial, cultural, and economic debates that occurred Detroit in the 1940s and 1950s as residents grappled with the numerous implications of the New Deal. It is not surprising that this debate would occur in a place like Detroit. The city was remade by the New Deal and war. The formerly heavily white, open-shop town was transformed into a labor bastion with a rapidly growing African American community. Almost immediately after the war ended, Detroiters fought (sometimes literally) to shape the political landscape of the city. In both the 1945 mayoral election and the 1946 gubernatorial campaign, voters grappled with the issue of labor's power and its political agenda. Detroiters battled over the extent to which labor would control local government and how much the welfare state would increase. Both of these questions grew directly out of the New Deal, which had empowered organized labor and expanded the welfare state. Opponents of New Deal liberalism articulated an antitax, libertarian philosophy. They argued that labor was too powerful and that unions used their influence in ways that were often detrimental to the public good, as when they demanded higher wages or called for higher taxes to support an expanded welfare state. During these elections, conservatives equated organized labor with Communism, a not-altogether wrong equation. Communists, after all, had played a crucial role in organizing the early unions, and they continued to play key roles in union leadership in the years after the war.

Detroiters also clashed over racial issues, which arose as a result of the enormous migration of African Americans to northern cities during World War II. In both the 1945 and 1949 mayoral elections, a majority of voters in both contests believed that integrationists threatened the city, and they conflated Communism with support for integration. As with labor, this was not a far-fetched equation. Communists had been at the forefront of the fight for civil rights throughout the late 1920s and 1930s. In 1949, white Detroiters particularly objected to using federal money to build public housing in outlying neighborhoods, which could potentially desegregate the city. Almost two-thirds of Detroit's white residents, including union members, supported segregated housing. They elected Albert Cobo, who portrayed himself as the protector of single-family homes against an intrusive federal government. Thus, in one of the most heavily prounion cities in the nation, voters backed a candidate who supported smaller, less activist government. As the welfare state became racialized, Detroit's white voters supported antigovernment conservatives. White Detroiters brought this ideology with them as they flocked to suburbs during the 1950s.

White homeowners were not the only group that articulated a small-government philosophy during the Cold War. American business leaders had long opposed an activist government, and businessmen like the DuPonts insisted throughout the 1930s that government intervention in the economy would destroy American liberty. However, during the first four decades of the twentieth century, this antistatist view had been an ideology of the elite. Many workers viewed American capitalism with great suspicion, particularly during the Great Depression, and they eagerly threw their support behind the economic reforms of the New Deal.

During the 1940s and 1950s, some Michigan businessmen, like many of their peers around the country, set out to reshape the political landscape. Executives during these years peppered their writings and speeches with diatribes against collectivism, planned economies, and Communism. However, they spent little time discussing the Soviet Union or the Communist Party when they warned against the collectivist threat. For most Detroit businessmen, the face of collectivism was UAW President Walter Reuther and Governor G. Mennan Williams, not Josef Stalin. They expressed far more concern with labor's size and the state's power than they did with the Kremlin. Businessmen during the early Cold War very effectively argued that the CIO had become too powerful and that it acted only in labor's selfish interests. Business rather than labor, they claimed, acted in the larger public welfare. State intervention in the economy, they argued, would make the economy less productive and would inevitably lead to totalitarianism. As businesses fled the high taxes and wages of the city and the state during the 1950s, this libertarian ideology made sense to an increasing number of Detroit-area residents. By the mid-1960s, limited government and free-market economics would no longer be an ideology of just the elite.

Detroit's Catholics expressed a far different view of the world. Catholics during the 1940s and 1950s argued that secularism undermined the foundations of Christian civilization. Catholics sought to reinfuse traditional values into the culture of Detroit residents, especially on the subject of family and gender. By the end of the 1950s, the large Catholic family with a working father and a stay-at-home mother had become the accepted model of the American family. Even when the reality of women working outside of the home did not match the ideal, the majority of Detroit-area women embraced their roles as wives and mothers. The Virgin Mary replaced Rosie the Riveter as the model women should emulate. When this 1950s-style patriarchal family was challenged decades later with the Equal Rights Amendment and *Roe v. Wade,* prominent conservative Catholics like Phyllis Schlafly were in the forefront of the anti-ERA and antiabortion movements.

By the late 1940s, Catholic critics of Communism could argue that Soviet actions in Eastern Europe violated American foreign policy values, especially self-determination against a totalitarian regime. Any American Communist supporters in the U.S. government thus also threatened core American foreign-policy ideals. This placed Catholics in a very different situation than they had been when the church expressed its anti-Communism by backing General Franco during the Spanish Civil War. Catholics demanded that the Soviet Union be stopped by framing their rhetoric in the ideology of the Atlantic Charter rather than the papal encyclicals. This language helped Catholics infuse their anti-Communism into the larger discourse of the early Cold War. They framed the fight against Communism as a battle between good and evil in which Communism and Catholicism were engaged in an eschatological confrontation. When Ronald Reagan stated many years later, "I have always maintained that the struggle now going on for the world will never be decided by bombs and rockets, or armies or military might. The real crisis we face today is a spiritual one; at root it is the test of moral will and faith," he was reiterating a worldview that was central to conservative Catholics.[2]

In this study of Cold War Detroit, we thus see the roots of contemporary conservatism, which combined support for free-market capitalism, small domestic government, anti-Communism, and traditionalism. All of these core ideas had been present in American society before the Cold War. The anti-Communism of the early Cold War helped bring together these previously disparate forces. Although the proponents of what became the new conservative movement did not always see eye-to-eye, they perceived that they shared common enemies. It would take many years and a great deal of both elite and grassroots activism before a powerful conservative movement formed nationally. That story is beyond the scope of this study. However, the components of that ideology were well developed long before the late 1960s and 1970s.

Anti-Communism during the Cold War galvanized political formation. Communism served as a screen on which Americans projected their fears—fears of statism, of racial integration, and of secularism. Particularly perplexing was the vehemence of the antistatist agenda, which seemed to undercut the economic security of those who voted for antistatist policies. The fact that so many different groups employed anti-Communist language made the 1950s seem in retrospect to have been a period of political consensus. However, many of the same issues that fractured American politics from the 1960s through the 1980s—civil rights, gender roles, deregulation, and conservative Christianity—were all central to the anti-Communism of the early Cold War.

With the end of the Cold War, American anti-Communism began to fade from public memory. As Richard Gid Powers pointed out, anti-Communism continued to live on "only in the bitter memory of those wounded during the long struggle." The scholars who celebrate "those wounded during the long struggle," according to Powers, have argued that the Soviet Union's collapse did not validate anti-Communist beliefs or actions. As a result, Powers says, "What the great majority of responsible anticommunists had really thought, what their role in American life really had been, all had been dropped from the historical record."[3] I hope that this book has helped illuminate what American anti-Communists believed. For many Americans, anti-Communism was the legitimate expression of deeply held beliefs about dangers the nation faced. For many conservatives during the Cold War, this threat came from abroad. But often the threat came from within as they worried that American society was becoming too secular and socialistic. At the same time, it is important to recognize that many liberals opposed Communism for their own legitimate reasons. While this opposition sometimes weakened liberalism, it made sense in the political and social context of the time.

Even though the fall of the Berlin Wall more than two decades ago signaled the end of organized Communism, Americans still respond to perceived political dangers of the welfare state using Cold-War-era language. Barack Obama's election and the expansion of government that occurred during the first years of his term saw a return to this old rhetoric. Once again, the real target of these "anti-Communists" was the welfare state, not the Communist Party. The rhetoric of anti-Communism has outlived Communism itself.

NOTES

INTRODUCTION

1. Nicholas Schorn, "Why the Block Rosary," *Our Lady of the Cape*, February 1952, 7–10; *Michigan Catholic*, April 10, 1952, 5.

2. B. E. Hutchinson, Chairman of the Finance Committee, Chrysler, "A United Front for Business" *Detroiter*, January 9, 1950, 7.

3. Patrick Allitt, *The Conservatives: Ideas and Personalities Throughout American History* (New Haven: Yale University Press, 2009), 173.

4. Gary Gerstle, "Race and the Myth of the Liberal Consensus," *Journal of American History* 82, no. 2 (September 1995): 579; Trilling quote from Leo Ribuffo, "Conservatism and American Politics," *Journal of the Historical Society* 3, no. 2 (Spring 2003): 165.

5. Alan Brinkley, "The Problem of American Conservatism," *American Historical Review* 99, no. 2 (April 1994): 409.

6. Matthew D. Lassiter, *The Silent Majority: Suburban Politics in the Sunbelt South* (Princeton, N.J.: Princeton University Press, 2007).

7. Thomas J. Sugrue, *The Origins of the Urban Crisis: Race and Inequality in Postwar Detroit* (Princeton, N.J.: Princeton University Press, 1996).

8. Lisa McGirr, *Suburban Warriors: The Origins of the New American Right* (Princeton, N.J.: Princeton University Press, 2002), 10–12.

9. Kim Phillips-Fein, *Invisible Hands: The Making of the Conservative Movement from the New Deal to Reagan* (New York: Norton, 2009); Elizabeth Tandy Shermer, "Origins of the Conservative Ascendancy: Barry Goldwater's Early Senate Career and the De-legitimization of Organized Labor," *Journal of American History* (December 2008): 678–709.

10. Allan J. Lichtman, *White Protestant Nation: The Rise of the American Conservative Movement.* (New York: Atlantic Monthly Press, 2008), 2.

11. Patrick Allitt, *The Conservatives: Ideas and Personalities throughout American History* (New Haven, Conn.: Yale University Press, 2009), 173.

12. As David M. Kennedy has argued, the late 1930s saw the emergence of "the

first systematic expressions of antigovernment political philosophy [which] had deep roots in American political culture but only an inchoate existence before the New Deal." These years marked a critical turning point in the history of twentieth-century conservatism. "The crystallization of this new conservative ideology, as much as the New Deal that precipitated its articulation, was among the enduring legacies of the 1930s." David M. Kennedy, *Freedom from Fear: The American People in Depression and War, 1929–1945* (New York: Oxford University Press, 1999), 341.

13. Julian E. Zelizer, "Rethinking the History of American Conservatism," *Reviews in American History* 38, no. 2 (2010): 388.

14. According to Berenice Baldwin, an FBI informer and Communist Party membership secretary, almost every industrial center in the state of Michigan had a Communist cell. The party had sixty-seven active cells in the Detroit area in 1947. John J. Najduch, "Red Strength in Detroit Outlined 5 Years Ago," *Detroit News,* February 27, 1952. For more on the Detroit Loyalty Program, see chapter 1.

15. As Morton Keller argues, "We can see that what emerged from the New Deal and World War Two was not xenophobia and standpattism (Japanese-American internment and segregated armed forces to the contrary notwithstanding). Rather, the basic New Deal themes of a broad, inclusive, democratic cultural nationalism, and a readiness to use federal programs and deficit financing when necessary to secure prosperity and meet large domestic or international needs, turned out to be the primary characteristics of American public life during the second half of the twentieth century." Morton Keller, "The New Deal: A New Look," *Polity* (Summer 1999): 660.

16. Eric Arnesen, "No 'Graver Danger': Black Anticommunism, the Communist Party, and the Race Question," *Labor: Studies in Working-Class History of the Americas* 3 (Winter 2006): 19–20; Manfred Berg, "Black Civil Rights and Liberal Anticommunism: The NAACP in the Early Cold War," *Journal of American History* (June 2007): 75–96.

17. The membership statistics are from the 1950 Official Catholic Directory and are quoted in *Michigan Catholic,* June 1, 1950, 1. While 70 percent of Catholics attended Mass at least once a week during the 1950s, only one-third of Protestants attended weekly services. Gerhard Lenski, *The Religious Factor: A Sociological Study of Religion's Impact on Politics, Economics, And Family Life* (Garden City, N.Y.: Doubleday, 1961), 34. The total population of the Detroit urbanized area was 2,659,398. United States Bureau of the Census, *United States Census of Population: 1950,* vol. 2, *Characteristics of the Population,* pt. 22, Michigan (Washington, D.C.): GPO, 1952. The boundaries of the archdiocese and the urbanized area as defined by the census do not correspond.

Chapter 1. New Deal Detroit, Communism, and Anti-Communism

1. Reynolds Farley, Sheldon Danziger, Harry H. Holzer, *Detroit Divided: A Volume in the Multi-City Study of Urban Inequality* (New York: Sage, 2000), 27.

2. Thomas A. Klug, "Labor Market Politics in Detroit: The Curious Case of the

'Spolansky Act' of 1931," *Michigan Historical Review* 14, no. 1 (Spring, 1988): 1–32.

3. Olivier Zunz, *The Changing Face of Inequality: Urbanization, Industrial Development, and Immigrants in Detroit, 1880–1920* (Chicago: University of Chicago Press, 1982), 292–309.

4. UAW membership statistics are from Nelson Lichtenstein, *Labor's War at Home: The CIO in World War II*, 80.

5. Robert Conot, *American Odyssey: A History of a Great City* (Detroit: Wayne State University Press, 1986), 393.

6. B. J. Widick, *Detroit: City of Race and Class Violence* (Detroit: Wayne State University, 1989), 47–53.

7. Walter S. Dunn, "Life as a Communist! Walter S. Dunn's Own Story," *Detroit News*, March 2, 1952. Dunn testified before HUAC when it came to Detroit in 1952. Of all the "friendly" former party members who appeared before the committee in Detroit, Dunn was the only non-spy.

8. Harvey Klehr, *The Heyday of American Communism: The Depression Decade*, (New York: Basic, 1984), 233.

9. Harvey Levenstein, *Communism, Anticommunism and the CIO* (Westport, Conn.: Greenwood, 1981), 52.

10. Roger Keeran, *The Communist Party and the Auto Workers Unions* (Bloomington: Indiana University Press, 1980).

11. Lewis quote in Robert H. Ziegler, *The CIO: 1935–1955* (Chapel Hill: University of North Carolina Press, 1995), 83.

12. Klehr, *Heyday of American Communism*, 380; Maurice Isserman, *Which Side Where You On? The American Communist Party during the Second World War* (Middletown, Conn.: Wesleyan University Press, 1982), 18–19.

13. The CRC was formed in 1946 in a merger between the International Labor Defense and the National Federation for Constitutional Liberties. The National Negro Congress became the National Negro Labor Council in 1951.

14. The Martinsville Seven were seven young black men who were convicted for a 1949 rape of a white woman in Virginia. They were found guilty and sentenced to death by electrocution, a punishment that stunned the local black community. Willie McGee, a black man from Mississippi, was convicted of raping a white woman despite evidence that they had been having a relationship for four years. McGee was also found guilty and sentenced to death after a trial that lasted one day.

15. M. J. Heale, *McCarthy's Americans: Red Scare Politics in State and Nation, 1935–1965* (Athens: University of Georgia Press, 1998), 86.

16. Alex Baskin, "The Ford Hunger March—1932," *Labor History* 13, no.3: 334; Ford quoted in Widick, *Detroit*, 48.

17. Quoted in Klug, "Labor Market Politics in Detroit," 21.

18. Baskin, "Ford Hunger March," 331–60.

19. Quoted in Heale, *McCarthy's Americans*, 91.

20. Quoted in Nelson Lichtenstein, *The Most Dangerous Man in Detroit: Walter Reuther and the Fate of American Labor*, (New York: Basic, 1995), 89.

21. Conot, *American Odyssey*, 366; Heale, *McCarthy's Americans*, 92.

22. Steven Fraser, *Labor Will Rule: Sidney Hillman and the Rise of American Labor* (New York: Free Press, 1991), 417.

23. Anders Geoffery Lewis, "Labor's Cold War: The AFL and Liberal Anticommunism" (PhD diss., University of Florida, 2000), 161.

24. Zieger, *The CIO*, 98.

25. At this point, the total UAW-CIO membership was about 350,000. Conot, *American Odyssey*, 367.

26. Robert H. Zieger, *The CIO*, 99; Fraser, *Labor Will Rule*, 416–20.

27. Duffy and Frey quoted in Lewis, "Labor's Cold War," 116–18.

28. Lewis, "Labor's Cold War," 116–18.

29. As Martin Halpern has pointed out, "Most participants in the Reuther group, to be sure, were to the left of the center of the American political spectrum. In UAW terms, however, the Reuther group was a center-right coalition." Martin Halpern, *UAW Politics in the Cold War Era* (Albany: State University of New York Press, 1988), 26.

30. Lichtenstein, *Most Dangerous Man*, 157.

31. Lichtenstein, *Most Dangerous Man*, 177–84.

CHAPTER 2. LABOR AND THE BIRTH
OF THE POSTWAR RED SCARE

1. Dorothy A. Riis, "Communists Gain," *Detroit News*, October 7, 1945, 6.

2. Shermer, "Origins," 678; Kim Phillips-Fein, *Invisible Hands*.

3. Lichtenstein, *Labor's War at Home*, 71-81.

4. UAW membership statistics are from Lichtenstein, *Labor's War at Home*, 80.

5. Statistic quoted in Nelson Lichtenstein, *State of the Union: A Century of American Labor* (Princeton, N.J.: Princeton University Press, 2002), 100.

6. "Detroit People in Perspective: A Survey of Group Attitudes and Aspirations," Office of War Information, Rensis Likert Papers, Box 9, Reports & Memoranda Folder, Section III, 4, Bentley Historical Library, University of Michigan.

7. While the AFL outnumbered the CIO nationally, the latter was by far the larger labor organization in Detroit. By 1945, the CIO had three hundred fifty thousand members in the city, while the AFL had only one hundred thousand. Conot, *American Odyssey*, 393.

8. Statistics on identification with workers are from Likert Papers, Box 9, Folder 9-39, Sec. III, p. 25. Interview with Store Room order filler at Briggs, Rensis Likert Papers, Box 25, Interviews, Office of War Information: Reports & Memoranda Folder, Bentley Historical Library, University of Michigan.

9. Interview with Machine Operator at Ford, Rensis Likert Papers, Box 25, Interviews, Office of War Information: Reports & Memoranda Folder, Bentley Historical Library, University of Michigan.

10. Rensis Likert Papers, Box 9, Office of War Information: Reports & Memo-

randa Folder, Bentley Historical Library, University of Michigan, Part IV, Section XII: Illustrative Appendix: Twenty Typical Detroiters and Four Veterans of World War I; Interview with Veteran of the Last War—Native Fascist, 150.

11. Interview with Clerk for OEM, Rensis Likert Papers, Box 25, Interviews, Office of War Information: Reports & Memoranda Folder, Bentley Historical Library, University of Michigan.

12. Rensis Likert Papers, Box 9, Office of War Information: Reports & Memoranda Folder, Bentley Historical Library, University of Michigan, Section III, 27.

13. "The interviewers were asked to designate each person interviewed by his chief antagonisms toward economic groups in the community." Rensis Likert Papers, Box 9, Office of War Information: Reports & Memoranda Folder, Bentley Historical Library, University of Michigan, Section III, 24, Table 24. Chief antagonisms toward economic groups.

14. Interview with plant engineer at Nash-Kelvinator (former salesman), Rensis Likert Papers, Box 25, Interviews, Office of War Information: Reports & Memoranda Folder, Bentley Historical Library, University of Michigan.

15. Rensis Likert Papers, Box 9, Office of War Information: Reports & Memoranda Folder, Bentley Historical Library, University of Michigan, Part IV, Section XII: Illustrative Appendix: Twenty Typical Detroiters and Four Veterans of World War I; Interview with Small Business—One Who Began in Business, 46. The city's economic divisions extended to its newspapers. According to the survey, executives, professionals, small-business owners, and white-collar workers were far more likely to read the *Detroit News*. Factory workers and service workers were more likely to read the *Detroit Times*, although a substantial number of them also read the *News*. "Table 4—Principal Detroit Newspapers Read."

16. Rensis Likert Papers, Box 9, Office of War Information: Reports & Memoranda Folder, Bentley Historical Library, University of Michigan, Part IV, Section XII: Illustrative Appendix: Twenty Typical Detroiters and Four Veterans of World War I; Interview with Executive—One of Largest Companies, Part IV, Section XII, 5.

17. Rensis Likert Papers, Box 9, Office of War Information: Reports & Memoranda Folder, Bentley Historical Library, University of Michigan, Part IV, Section XII: Illustrative Appendix: Twenty Typical Detroiters and Four Veterans of World War I; Interview with Veteran of the Last War—Native Fascist, 150.

18. This chapter will discuss labor and chapter 3 will discuss race and anti-Communism.

19. *New York Times*, October 21, 1945.

20. In addition, Jeffries had alienated many Democrats with his attack on FDR and support for Dewey in the 1944 election. The Detroit mayor was a nonpartisan position, and mayors were not supposed to take such partisan stands.

21. Frankensteen quoted this from Jeffries's pamphlet and complained about the Mayor's "smear campaign." "Frankensteen Hits at 'Smear Campaign'," *Detroit News*, October 19, 1945. A subsequent version of this pamphlet was printed in the *Detroit News* that showed a hairy hand above a picture of the city. The text read: "Beware!

Outside interests have launched a powerful plot to seize the government of the City of Detroit from the hands of the people, to use for their own selfish interests. . . . Their all-out objective is to use Detroit as a lever to force through their pet ideas of social and economical revolution on a national basis. They are crusading for a nation-wide upheaval. The welfare of Detroit does not hold No. 1 Priority with them. Keep your city government where it belongs—in the hands of the people. Keep your City Hall at Home. Re-elect Mayor Jeffries." *Detroit News*, November 2, 1945.

22. "Frankensteen Tells His Mayoral Goal," *Detroit News*, October 10, 1945.

23. Jeffries quoted in Carl O. Smith and Stephen B. Sarasohn, "Hate Propaganda in Detroit," *Public Opinion Quarterly* (Spring 1946): 43.

24. "Candidates Dispute PAC Campaign Role," *Detroit News*, October 18, 1945.

25. "A Political Strike," *Detroit News*, October 2, 1945.

26. Bob Jones, "Wants to Work," *Detroit News*, October 4, 1945.

27. Letter from E. R., "Who Runs It?" *Detroit News*, October 6, 1945.

28. Letter from J. J. Appenzeller, "Freeze Everything," *Detroit News*, October 6, 1945.

29. One of the most prominent conservative, antilabor voices during the 1945 campaign was Floyd McGriff, the editor of numerous westside and suburban community newspapers. McGriff took an even more conspiratorial view of why labor acted so selfishly. Communists, McGriff claimed, were behind some of the biggest Detroit-area strikes, particularly the dispute at the Kelsey-Hayes Wheel Company. The strike began, according to McGriff, when two Communist supporters were fired for ejecting an unpopular foreman from the plant. Communist leaders in the local vowed to strike Kelsey-Hayes, despite the company's "key position in reconversion work," until it promised to rehire the discharged men. McGriff contended that such an action reflected "the first principle of Communist strategy—keep a plant tied up whenever any communist or fellow traveler is in trouble. It does not matter how many innocent bystanders, or how many union men not in sympathy with the deal are involved." Communist leaders in the CIO, McGriff charged, acted in the party's narrow interests, regardless of the cost to workers or the public.

According to McGriff's newspapers, Frankensteen's election was part of this larger Communist campaign. Communists, McGriff claimed, recognized that a "rebellion is brewing against the Stalinists in the Detroit area among the rank and file." In order to preserve their power, McGriff argued, party members in Detroit had used their control of the CIO's Wayne County Council to push fellow traveler Richard Frankensteen into the mayoral campaign over the objections of anti-Communist CIO leaders. Once Frankensteen was elected, the party would no longer have to worry that their CIO opponents would put them out of office, since "Detroit will be the first big city with the city hall in their [CP's] pocket." Joe Zack, former member of the National Executive Board of the CPUSA, "Inside Story of Control by Communists on Policy," *Redford Record*, September 13, 1945.

30. "Frankensteen Tells His Mayoral Goal," *Detroit News*, October 10, 1945. Frankensteen also had to defend himself against charges that he was a Communist.

He ran large ads in the *Detroit News* pledging that he was not a Communist and would not appoint any Communists to city office if he were elected. "This is My Solemn Pledge!" *Detroit News*, November 1, 1945.

31. "Reconversion Fight with CIO Imminent," *Detroit Labor News*, June 8, 1945.

32. "Federation Backs Jeffries," *Detroit Labor News*, October 12, 1945.

33. "Vote AFL, Nov. 6," *Detroit Labor News*, October 26, 1945.

34. Traditionally, AFL affiliates had followed Samuel Gompers's belief that "What the law gives or what the state gives, the state can take away. But what you get through your own exertions you can hold as long as you maintain your strength." But, as Andrew Kersten has pointed out, "The Second World War became a watershed when the AFL finally realized that economic security and stability would come only with an alliance with the federal government." Andrew E. Kersten, *Labor's Home Front: The American Federation of Labor During World War II* (New York: New York University Press, 2006), 3. During World War II, the AFL somewhat reluctantly agreed to work in a tripartite system. However, at the end of the war, AFL leaders like AFL President William Green repeatedly insisted that "industrial peace will be attained in America only through organization and through free collective bargaining." Green argued, "The great need of the post-war period will be to prevail upon the Government to surrender controls over collective bargaining—not to increase them." William Green, "Federal Regulations Threatens Strangulation of Labor Unions," *Detroit Labor News*, August 31, 1945; Gompers quoted in Thaddeus Russell, *Out of the Jungle: Jimmy Hoffa and the Remaking of the American Working Class* (New York: Knopf, 2001), 54.

35. "Relate Frankensteen's Background as Union Official," *Redford Record*, September 27, 1945.

36. "Teamsters Union Tells Why It Backs Jeffries," *Redford Record*, November 1, 1945, 19.

37. One element of this "radical" agenda was the possibility that Frankensteen would support policies to integrate white neighborhoods. Race and anti-Communism will be discussed in more detail in Chapter 3.

38. In the primary, Frankensteen received 44 percent, Jeffries 37 percent, and Friel 19 percent. Friel campaigned for Frankensteen before the final election. Smith and Sarasohn, "Hate Propaganda in Detroit," 47.

39. In fact, the local elections that saw the greatest turnouts—1937, 1943, and 1945—were all years when the CIO supported one of the candidates. Sixty-four percent of registered voters participated in the final election. The highest percentage was 67 percent in 1937. Smith and Sarasohn, "Hate Propaganda in Detroit," 26–27.

40. Smith and Sarasohn divided these "Native White Neighborhoods" into five classes based on the residents' socioeconomic status. The support for Jeffries in the four most affluent neighborhoods ranged between 82 percent and 67 percent. The "Native White Class V" supported Jeffries by 55 percent to 45 percent. Among immigrant voters, only the residents of the Irish neighborhood supported Jeffries. Smith and Sarasohn, "Hate Propaganda in Detroit," 48–50.

41. "The Peace is Won! Where Do We Go from Here?" *Detroit Labor News*, Aug. 17, 1945.

42. Theodore Rosenof, "Freedom, Planning and Totalitarianism: The Reception of F. A. Hayek's *Road to Serfdom*," *Canadian Review of American Studies* (Fall 1974): 157; Alan Brinkley, *The End of Reform: New Deal Liberalism in Recession and War*. New York: Vintage, 1995.

43. "The Full Employment Bill," *Detroit Labor News*, June 8, 1945.

44. As Andrew Kersten has pointed out, "Working with New Dealers did not mean that the AFL adopted all aspects of liberalism. Specifically, when confronted with federal demands for racial equality or gender equity, the AFL maintained its prewar ideology." Kersten, *Labor's Home Front*, xi. Race in particular remained a major point of contention within the labor movement and between Communists and anti-Communists during the 1940s and 1950s.

45. Public support for price controls fell from roughly 80 percent in May 1946 to 40 percent in October 1946. Meg Jacobs, "'How About Some Meat?': The Office of Price Administration, Consumption Politics, and State Building from the Bottom Up, 1941–1946," *Journal of American History* 84, no. 3 (December 1997): 939.

46. Gallup Poll, 606, 608.

47. "GOP Strength Is Growing," *Detroit News*, October 28, 1946.

48. Letter to the editor from William L. Moore, "CIO Follows the Russian Lead," *Detroit News*, October 6, 1946.

49. Quoted in Lichtenstein, *Most Dangerous Man*, 256.

50. Allitt, *The Conservatives*, 159–160; "The Road to Serfdom in Cartoons," *Look*, February 1945, available at http://mises.org/books/TRTS (accessed March 28, 2012).

51. "Democratic 'Bungling' is Assailed by Sigler," *Detroit News*, October 20, 1946.

52. *Ibid.*

53. *Ibid.*

54. Van Wagoner quoted in "Democratic 'Bungling'"; Sigler quoted in "Sigler Backs Bonus, Airport Proposals," *Detroit News*, October 22, 1946.

55. Florence Behenna, "Good Old GOP," (letter to the editor), *Detroit News*, November 2, 1946.

56. "Sigler Wins; Bonus Voted: State Gives GOP Slate Huge Lead," *Detroit News*, November 6, 1946.

57. Arnold J. Levin, "Van Wagoner Warns Labor to Hold Gains," *Detroit News*, October 28, 1946.

58. Letter to the editor from Raoul Barker, "Kiss of Death," *Detroit News*, October 31, 1946.

59. "Out Goes the New Deal!" *Detroit News*, November 6, 1946.

60. "Republicans Given Vast Responsibility," *Detroit News*, November 6, 1946.

61. Joseph Loftus, "Board Pledges CIO to U.S. Allegiance, Scorns Communism," *New York Times*, November 18, 1946.

62. Although the proposal did not call for any purges, it did create machinery

to "dislodge pro-Communist elements from positions of influence in the CIO and its constituent bodies." In addition, it limited the authority of CIO city and state councils, a number of which were dominated by the left. *New York Times*, December 1, 1946.

63. The CIO also found that its position on American foreign policy was being pushed toward anti-Communism. Its previous position of criticizing both the United States and Soviet Union for increasing international tension was no longer tenable in the developing Cold War environment of early 1947. In the crucial fifteen weeks between February 21, when the British informed the U.S. State Department that they could no longer give aid to Greece and Turkey, and June 5, when Secretary of State Marshall proposed what was to become the Marshall Plan, American foreign policy profoundly shifted. The American government announced its intention to fight Communism abroad and agreed to aid in the herculean task of rebuilding Europe in order to stave off Communist victories in war-ravaged European nations. In response to the Truman Doctrine and the Marshall Plan, both the AFL and the CIO answered the government's call to help rebuild Europe. State Department officials recognized that they needed American unions to participate because the war had thoroughly discredited European industrialists while enhancing the reputation of the European left. In order to win the battle between Communists and socialists within Western European labor, President Truman appointed two labor leaders—the CIO's James Carey and the AFL's George Meany—to the nineteen-member advisory committee that helped formulate the scope of the Marshall Plan and that helped whip up popular support. As the CIO threw its institutional backing behind the Marshall Plan, foreign policy issues became increasingly contentious within the organization. Pro–Marshall Plan unionists like Philip Murray and Walter Reuther argued that if labor did not back the plan, "there won't be any free trade unions anywhere in Europe, as there aren't any on the other side of the Iron Curtain." Pro-Soviet trade unionists were reticent to back a plan that would use American aid as a weapon with which to defeat European Communism. The Marshall Plan thus became an issue that drew anti-Communist labor leaders further into the orbit of the Truman administration while simultaneously making it difficult for these same leaders to abide by the presence of Communists and their allies within the CIO. Lichtenstein, *Most Dangerous Man*, 328–29; Zieger, *The CIO*, 264–66.

64. Foss Baker was later identified as a member of the Communist Party by Wayne Salisbury during Salisbury's testimony in front of HUAC in 1952. Salisbury had been a spy for the Michigan State Police in the Michigan Communist Party, of which he was a member from 1941 to 1948. Congress, House, Committee on Un-American Activities, *Communism in the Detroit Area—Part 1*, Hearing before the Committee on Un-American Activities, 82nd Cong., February 1952, testimony of Wayne Salisbury, 2833–2851.

65. Martha Biondi, *To Stand and Fight: The Struggle for Civil Rights in Postwar New York City* (Cambridge: Harvard University Press, 2003), 29.

66. "Congress Cracks Down on Reds," *Detroit Labor News*, June 21, 1946.

67. Sigler quoted in Heale, *McCarthy's Americans*, 108.

68. The letter from an unnamed Michigan citizen is in James Truett Selcraig, *The Red Scare in the Midwest, 1945–1955: A State and Local Study*, (UMI Research, 1982), 5.

69. Samuel A. Tower, "Cacchione Berates House Red Inquiry," *New York Times*, March 29, 1947.

70. "Thomas Denies Charge," *New York Times*, March 29, 1947.

71. Walter Reuther Collection, Box 143, Folder 4, Archives of Labor and Urban Affairs (ALUA), Wayne State University, Detroit.

72. The legislation that gutted the Workmen's Compensation Act was known as the Bonine-Tripp amendments to the Michigan labor law. Halpern, *UAW Politics*, 314–22; Dudley Buffa, *Union Power and American Democracy: The UAW and the Democratic Party, 1935–72* (Ann Arbor: University of Michigan Press, 1984), 12.

73. "MFL Urges Sigler's Veto of Labor Bills," *Detroit Labor News*, June 27, 1947.

74. Walter Reuther to Governor Kim Sigler, June 16, 1947. Walter Reuther Collection, Box 426, Folder 15, ALUA.

75. August Scholle, "Callahan Repeal Move Ill-Advised," reprinted from *Michigan CIO News*, August 20, 1947, WPR Collection, Box 579, Folder 4, ALUA.

76. Buffa, *Union Power*, 21. This restrictive legislation was being passed in Michigan at the same time that Congress was passing the Taft-Hartley Act.

77. In fact, during the 1930s and 1940s, Michigan Democrats had been largely unconcerned with actually winning state offices. As long as Democrats held power nationally, party leaders in Michigan controlled plenty of federal patronage positions. They worried that a Democratic governor or senator would take control over patronage away from the Michigan national committeeman. As a result, party leaders felt that they had little to gain and much to lose if a Democrat won the governorship or senate seat. The party thus concentrated on delivering the vote for president, not for state offices. The few successful state Democratic candidates, such as Frank Murphy or Murray Van Wagoner, won office with little support from the Michigan Democratic Party. Buffa, *Union Power*, 10–12.

78. Quote from CIO-PAC resolution adopted on March 13, 1948, Buffa, *Union Power*, 15.

79. At the same time that Scholle and the CIO-PAC were attempting to remake the state party into a vehicle for labor-liberalism, they were engaged in a vicious battle with Jimmy Hoffa and the Teamsters for control of the Michigan Democratic party. In June 1948, George Fitzgerald, a front man for the Teamsters, won the election for Democratic national committeeman. He thus became the Michigan Democratic Party's representative to the Democratic National Committee and the liaison with the White House. Fitzgerald's victory over the CIO-backed candidate gave Hoffa control of over four hundred federal patronage jobs in Michigan and a direct connection to the president. The latter would be particularly helpful in staving off federal prosecution against Hoffa and the Teamsters. For the next six years,

a vision of the Blessed Virgin while he was conducting the Inquisition against the Albigensian heretics. From the mid-nineteenth to the early twentieth centuries, the Rosary became a weapon in the fight against the church's new enemies, especially anticlerical liberalism and the expanding modern state. In Germany, for instance, a Marian apparition at Marpingen during the late nineteenth century coincided with the *Kulturkampf*, the attempt by Bismarck to crush the church's power and extend state control. In 1931, a Marian vision in Ezkioga in the Basque Country appeared just as the Spanish Second Republic had undertaken its campaign against the church. Hundreds of thousands of worshipers flocked to the sites of these visions and eagerly embraced Mary's call to pray the Rosary, despite the fact that the church hierarchy did not approve the apparitions at either Marpingen or Ezkioga. Marina Warner, *Alone of All Her Sex: The Myth and the Cult of the Virgin Mary* (New York: Vintage, 1983), 305–9; David Blackbourn, *Marpingen: Apparitions of the Virgin Mary in a Nineteenth-Century German Village* (New York: Vintage, 1993); William A. Christian, *Visionaries: the Spanish Republic and the reign of Christ* (Berkeley: University of California Press, 1996).

32. Although the vision at Fatima occurred in 1917, the cult did not become widely known until the early 1940s. Sandra L. Zimdars-Swartz, *Encountering Mary: From LaSalette to Medjugorje* (Princeton, N.J.: Princeton University Press, 1991), 68; "'Prayer, Penance, Miracle of Mary' World's Hope" *Michigan Catholic*, April 3, 1947, 3. The Blessed Virgin's message was repeated often in the diocesan paper. See, for example, *Michigan Catholic*, August 14, 1947, 4; October 16, 1947, 4; February 5, 1948, 4; March 25, 1948, 7; February 9, 1950, 4; May 4, 1950, 4.

33. Quote from Father Joseph L. Lilly, C.M., "Sees Red Tide Stemmed by Aid of Virgin Mary," *Michigan Catholic*, December 13, 1945; Warner, *Alone of All Her Sex*, 308.

34. Other Marian devotions had long been popular in Detroit. During the 1920s, for instance, thousands of Detroit Catholics flocked to novenas, or nine-day-long prayers, in honor of Our Lady of Lourdes, drawn, no doubt, by reports of miraculous cures at the grotto at Detroit's St. Mary's Church. During the Depression, novenas for the unemployed and needy drew thousands of venerators.

35. "Our Blessed Mother's Revelations to a Privileged Soul," *Fatima Rosary, Family Rosary, Block Rosary* newsletter from the Block Rosary Lay Apostolate, n.d., Blue Army of Fatima File, Chancery Collection, 1950–81, AAD.

36. Rather than attempting to view this apparition and the devotion that grew out of it in functionalist terms, I instead am following historian Robert Orsi's admonition to recognize that modern historiography lacks the language with which to discuss these moments when the "transcendent breaks into time." Orsi points out that "Western modernity exists under the sign of absence. Time and space are emptied of presence. . . . Drained of presence, religious experience is remade in conformity with modern liberal notions of what 'religion' is: autonomous, a distinct domain apart from other areas of life, private, in conformity with the causal laws of nature, reasonable, interior—all the things that Marian apparitions and what follows from

them are not." For devout Catholics like the housewife discussed above, "in the culture within which apparitions take place there is nothing out of the ordinary about them. . . . They are anticipated, longed for, even expected." Robert A. Orsi, "Abundant History: Marian Apparitions as Alternative Modernity," *Historically Speaking*, September/October 2008: 12–16.

37. "Newest Fatima Clubs Thrill 'Pioneer'," *Michigan Catholic*, October 30, 1947, 3. While the Church always viewed uninvestigated apparitions and miracles with a great deal of skepticism, it was loath to reject anything that increased devotion and religious participation. On the other hand, personal revelation potentially undermined the authority of the church. The Catholic Church during the Cold War was thus forced to walk a fine line between encouraging devotion to officially approved apparitions like Fatima while controlling and confining lay enthusiasm as much as possible. See undated letter from the Office of the Archdiocese, Edward Mooney Collection, AAD. Schorn's beliefs were similar to those expressed by conservative Catholic intellectuals, who saw the Cold War as an "eschatological struggle in which Christian Western civilization, the preserve of truth and faith, confronted a demonic nemesis." Patrick Allitt, *Catholic Intellectuals and Conservative Politics in America, 1950–1985* (Ithaca, Cornell University Press, 1993), 60. The "fertile soil" quote is from the American bishops statement on secularism, "Exclusion of God Root of World Woes," *Michigan Catholic*, November 20, 1947, 3.

38. Nicholas Schorn, "Why the Block Rosary," rough draft in Chancery Collection, Rosary Societies, AAD.

39. "They Recaptured May Day for Mary," *Michigan Catholic*, May 8, 1947, 1.

40. 1954 was the year when the pope named Mary Queen of Heaven. *Michigan Catholic*, May 27, 1954, 1–2; "15,000 Here Honor Mary on Her Day," *Michigan Catholic*, May 15, 1947.

41. Nicholas Schorn, "Why the Block Rosary?" *Our Lady of the Cape*, February 1952, 7–10.

42. "Block Rosary Group Thanks Anne Campbell," letter to the editor, *Michigan Catholic*, April 12, 1951, 4.

43. For a discussion of postwar expertise, see Brian Balogh, *Chain Reaction: Expert Debate and Public Participation in American Commercial Nuclear Power, 1945–1975* (New York: Cambridge University Press, 1991).

44. In the Detroit metropolitan area, 27 percent of women over age fourteen were employed outside of the home in 1950. GPO, *Census of the Population, 1950*, vol. 2, Characteristics of the Population, Part 22, Michigan, Table 35. Percentage is of women in the standard metropolitan area (SMA) of Detroit.

45. Text of speech by John J. Maher, state commander of the Catholic War Veterans, April 1947, Chancery Collection, Organizations and Societies, AAD.

46. Rev. Patrick Peyton, "Report on the Family Rosary," UDEV 13/13, Family Rosary; "The Story of the Family Rosary," COHA 10/08, Archives of the University of Notre Dame.

47. Text of speech by John J. Maher, state commander of the Catholic War Veterans, April 1947, Chancery Collection, Organizations and Societies, AAD.

48. In Detroit, the Archdiocesan Council of Catholic Men, a prominent lay group, spread the message of the family Rosary with their Radio Rosary Crusade. The council broadcast the Rosary over station WJLB from 7:15 to 7:30 every night in October, the month of the Holy Rosary. By 1950, the Council estimated that two hundred thousand Detroit area residents turned in to this program and joined in the Rosary recitation. "Annual Report of the Detroit Archdiocesan Council of Catholic Men for the Year Ending March 31, 1950," Edward Mooney Collection, AAD.

49. Rev. Patrick Peyton, "Report on the Family Rosary," UDEV 13/13, Family Rosary; "The Story of the Family Rosary," COHA 10/08, Archives of the University of Notre Dame.

50. Elaine Tyler May, *Homeward Bound: American Families in the Cold War Era* (New York: Basic, 1990), 11.

51. "Time for Rededication to Her Ideals," *Michigan Catholic*, May 12, 1955, 4.

52. *St. John's Bulletin*, September 12, 1948, AAD.

53. Archbishop Mooney was elevated to the College of Cardinals in 1946. Cardinal Mooney speech before the Marian Congress in Ottawa, "To Jesus through Mary!" *Michigan Catholic*, June 26, 1947, 5.

54. *St. Rose of Lima Messenger*, April 15, 1951, 1. These groups ranged in size from five to twenty people. *St. Rose of Lima Messenger*, November 27, 1953, 4.

55. *St. Rose of Lima Messenger*, August 24, 1952, 1.

56. Alice Therese Diehl, "Hearts Turn to Mary During Month of May," *Michigan Catholic*, April 21, 1949.

57. *1956 Detroit Area Study*, question 13: "Thinking of all the things you do, what are the things that make you feel useful?" Among Detroit Catholic nonworking women, 55.7 percent said that homemaking made them feel most useful and 18.6 percent said the same for childrearing. In comparison, only 39 percent of non-Catholic Detroit housewives celebrated homemaking and 11 percent claimed that childrearing was their most valuable accomplishment. A similar pattern existed for suburban women: 45.2 percent of Catholic suburban housewives claimed that homemaking made them feel most worthwhile and 28.6 percent claimed the same for childrearing, while 35.5 percent of non-Catholic suburban women embraced homemaking and 14.5 percent felt that childrearing was their most useful activity.

58. *1956 Detroit Area Study*, question 6a: "Thinking of all the things you do, what are the things that make you feel most important?" The pollsters asked employed women to answer this question and asked question thirteen of women who were not employed outside of the home. For working women, 23 percent of non-Catholic Detroit women answered that work made them feel most useful, compared with 16 percent of Catholics. For question 6a, the number of employed Catholic and non-Catholic suburban women was so small as to be almost statistically insignificant. However, 3 of 21 (14 percent) of working Catholic suburban women and 3 of 27

(11 percent) of non-Catholic suburban women answered that work or making a living made them feel most important.

59. According to the 1953 Detroit Area Study, 27 percent of the residents in the Detroit area had lived there all their lives, while 28 percent had moved to Detroit in the period from 1945 to early 1953. Detroit Area Study, *A Social Profile of Detroit: 1953*, (Institute for Social Research, University of Michigan: 1954), 13.

60. In reality, these ethnic neighborhoods had been far from completely Catholic. However, parishioners' cultural and spiritual lives so centered around the parish that Catholics often mistakenly reported that they lived in completely Catholic neighborhoods when in fact only 50 percent of the residents belonged to the church. John McGreevey, *Parish Boundaries: The Catholic Encounter with Race in the 20th Century Urban North* (Chicago: University of Chicago Press, 1996), 79.

61. Kathryn A. Johnson, "The Home Is a Little Church: Gender, Culture, and Authority in American Catholicism, 1940–1962," (PhD. diss., University of Pennsylvania, 1997), 18.

62. Tentler, *Seasons of Grace*, 358–59.

63. Fr. Hubert A. Maino, "The Parish: Focus and Factory of Our Fellowship in Christ," *Michigan Catholic*, January 11, 1951, 8.

64. Statistics quoted in Gerhard Lenski, *The Religious Factor: A Sociologist's Inquiry* (Garden City, N.Y.: Anchor, 1963), 41.

65. Robert Orsi, *Thank You, St. Jude: Women's Devotion to the Patron Saint of Lost Causes* (New Haven, Conn.: Yale University Press, 1996), 182–83.

66. Peter A. Huff, *Allen Tate and the Catholic Revival: Trace of the Fugitive Gods* (New York: Paulist, 1996), 10; Robert Orsi, *The Madonna of 115th Street: Faith and Community in Italian Harlem* (New Haven, Conn.: Yale University Press, 2002); Johnson, "Home is a Little Church."

67. For instance, according to Schorn, when "Mrs. E . . ." of an eastside Detroit parish formed a block Rosary, ten of the sixteen families who agreed to participate were Protestant. Schorn, "Why the Block Rosary?" 7–10. In an article about Schorn, he was quoted as stating, "The practice of rotating weekly meetings from home to home has created a mass religious consciousness, causing many who had been indifferent to return to the Sacraments. . . . In Detroit there has been a large number of baptisms of non-Catholics who joined Rosary groups." "Rosary Block Circles the World," *Michigan Catholic*, February 10, 1949, 2.

68. Donald T. Critchlow, *Phyllis Schlafly and Grassroots Conservatism: A Woman's Crusade* (Princeton, N.J.: Princeton University Press, 2005).

CHAPTER 5. BUSINESS, ANTI-COMMUNISM, AND THE WELFARE STATE

1. In contrast, net income for all U.S. corporations in 1929 was $9 billion before federal taxes, and in 1941 it was $14.5 billion. "War, Cash, and Corporations: Prof-

its Have Been Good (Even after High Taxes), Dividends Have Been Low, and U.S. Business Has the Biggest Bank Account in History," *Fortune*, April 1945: 114–269.

2. The GM Post-war Planning Policy Group was created by Alfred P. Sloan, GM Chairman, to "plan for the post-war period" in a way that would enable GM to meet the needs of the stockholders and to "measure up to the standards of past [GM] accomplishment." Letter from Donaldson Brown to GM Post-War Planning Policy Group, January 11, 1943, Brown Collection, Box 1, Hagley Museum and Library. Howell Harris, *The Right to Manage: Industrial Relations Policies of American Business in the 1940s* (Madison: University of Wisconsin Press, 1982), 188–89; Brinkley, *End of Reform*.

3. Rosenof, "Freedom, Planning and Totalitarianism," 157; Brinkley, *End of Reform*.

4. A number of historians have discussed this postwar battle between business and the labor-liberal left. Peter Irons, for instance, argued that businessmen used anti-Communism to red bait their leftist opponents into submission. Executives, according to Irons, exaggerated the threat posed by the Soviet Union and domestic radicals in order to "cripple trade union strength and liberalism in general." Irons argues that this anti-Communist campaign was directed by "zealots possessing an apocalyptic view of Communism and an unremitting zeal to defeat the Soviet Union and its American supporters." Peter H. Irons, "American Business and the Origins of McCarthyism: The Cold War Crusade of the United States Chamber of Commerce," in *The Specter: Original Essays on the Cold War and the Origins of McCarthyism*, edited by Robert Griffith and Athan Theoharis, 77–78 (New York: New Viewpoints, 1974); Robert Griffith, "Forging America's Postwar Order: Domestic Politics and Political Economy in the Age of Truman" in *The Truman Presidency*, edited by Michael J. Lacey, 57–88 (New York: Cambridge University Press, 1991); Howell Harris and Elizabeth Fones-Wolf argue that businessmen feared the continued expansion of New Deal government and sought to recapture the "right to manage." See Harris, *The Right to Manage*, and Fones-Wolf, *Selling Free Enterprise: The Business Assault on Labor and Liberalism, 1945–1960* (Urbana: University of Illinois Press, 1994); Kim Phillips-Fein, *Invisible Hands*.

5. Address by Herbert R. Dusendorf, Purchasing Agent, Nelson Company, Detroit before the 1950 Spring Meeting of the Central Supply Association, *Detroiter*, November 13, 1950, 6.

6. Fones-Wolf, *Selling Free Enterprise*.

7. Mark Leff, "The Politics of Sacrifice on the American Home Front in World War II," *Journal of American History*, March 1991: 1296–318; Brinkley, *End of Reform*, 147.

8. United States Department of Agriculture, "Detroit People in Perspective: A Survey of Group Attitudes and Aspirations," Part IV, Section XII: Illustrative Appendix: Twenty Typical Detroiters and Four Veterans of World War I, Interview with Veteran of the Last War—Native Fascist, 147; Interview with Small Business—One

Who Began in Business, 48; Interview with Veteran of the Last War—Native Fascist, 150. Rensis Likert Papers, Box 9, Office of War Information: Reports & Memoranda Folder, Bentley Historical Library, University of Michigan.

9. Letter from Donaldson Brown to GM Post-War Planning Policy Group, January 11, 1943, Brown Collection, Box 1, Hagley Museum and Library.

10. According to a 1942 survey of Detroit, "[C]ertain government activities which are disliked by other occupational groups as encroachments barely tolerable for the sake of the war, large numbers of factory workers say they would like to see continued after the war, such as price and rent control." Rensis Likert Papers, Box 9, Office of War Information: Reports & Memoranda Folder, Bentley Historical Library, University of Michigan, Section III h. "Changing Concepts of the Role of the Federal Government," 141.

11. Thomas Lifka, *The Concept "Totalitarianism" and American Foreign Policy, 1933–1949* (New York: Garland, 1988).

12. Congress, House, Special Committee on Post-War Economic Policy and Planning, *Post-War Economic Policy and Planning Part 1: Contract Termination and Related Matters*, 78th Cong., 2nd Sess., March 22, 1944, 71; "A Lesson of the War," General Motors Corporation, Annual Report 1945, 22.

13. Alfred Sloan to Walter S. Carpenter Jr., November 16, 1945, quoted in Lichtenstein, *Most Dangerous Man*, 230.

14. General Motors Corporation, *1946 Annual Report*, 19.

15. "The Road to Serfdom in Cartoons," reproduced from a booklet published by General Motors, Detroit, in the "Thought Starter" series (no. 118). Published in *Look*, 1945, available at http://mises.org/books/TRTS/ (accessed March 28, 2012); Donaldson Brown, Vice Chairman, GM, "Problems of Industrial Organization and Control" speech presented before the Chicago Chapter of Society for Advancement of Management, November 16, 1945, Brown Collection, Box 5, Hagley. See Fones-Wolf, *Selling Free Enterprise*, 2.

16. George H. Gallup, *The Gallup Poll: Public Opinion 1935–1971*, 551. Between December 7 and December 12, 1945, the Gallup Poll asked, "Do you think workers at General Motors should get more pay?" Sixty percent said yes while only 22 percent said no.

17. "Rising Threat of Auto Strike Casts Pall Over All Detroit," *New York Times*, November 19, 1945.

18. "Ford Outlines 'Industrial Faith'; Asks Union-Employer Cooperation," *New York Times*, January 10, 1946.

19. George Romney, general manager of the Automobile Manufacturers Association, quote in "Romney Declares Reuther Falsifier," *New York Times*, June 23, 1946.

20. Lichtenstein, *Most Dangerous Man*, 220–47; Jacobs, "'How About Some Meat?'" 937–38.

21. Not all NAM members supported this new public-relations strategy. Chrysler's B. E. Hutchinson, long-time NAM activist and former Liberty Leaguer, attacked a pamphlet written by NAM staff members that reflected the new strategy. Andrew

Workman, "Manufacturing Power: The Organizational Revival of the National Association of Manufacturers, 1941–1945," *Business History Review* 72 (Summer 1998): 293.

22. Workman, "Manufacturing Power." Corporate liberal historians like Kim McQuaid and Thomas Ferguson argue that the organized business community was not unified and that the more moderate business associations continued to set the agenda. McQuaid and Ferguson see a split between older, labor-intensive businesses on the one hand and capital-intensive industries and their allies in international finance on the other. The latter, they argue, shaped American domestic and foreign policy from the New Deal until the 1970s. Firms such as Standard Oil and General Electric used their influence to defeat the agenda of labor-intensive industries during the New Deal. The latter had traditionally supported high protective tariffs, an isolationist foreign policy, and fierce antilabor domestic strategies. In comparison, capital-intensive firms supported limited labor reform because unionism was relatively cheap for their businesses. They chafed at restrictive tariffs because their businesses were powerful enough to compete in the world market and win. According to McQuaid and Ferguson, leaders of capital-intensive firms and the foundations these firms supported—men such as Paul Hoffman, Charles E. Wilson of GE, Beardsley Ruml, and Averell Harriman—shaped the key legislation of the New Deal through such associational organizations as the Business Advisory Council and the Council for Economic Development. After World War II, these same industries shaped American policy to create both an open, liberal world trade system and a labor-management accord because they recognized that their firms were strong enough to emerge victorious in such a system. Howell Harris, however, has argued persuasively that the business community was far more unified in its opinions on labor and that the NAM rather than the CED set the agenda on labor policy. This was certainly the case during the Taft-Hartley debate. Thomas Ferguson, "From Normalcy to New Deal: Industrial Structure, Party Competition, and American Public Policy in the Great Depression," *International Organization* 38, no. 1 (Winter 1984): 41–94; Kim McQuaid, *Uneasy Partners: Big Business in American Politics, 1945–1990* (Baltimore, 1994); Howell John Harris, *The Right to Manage,* 119–20.

23. Anthony Leviero, "Wilson, Green Say Labor Is Bending toward Socialism," *New York Times,* January 22, 1947; "Industry-Wide Bargaining Hit by Emery," *Pulling Together: Bulletin of the Small Business Men's Association,* June 1947, 3. Small-business owners particularly opposed industry-wide bargaining. Dewitt Emery, president of the Small Business Men's Association, pointed out that under such a scenario, a union's national headquarters would negotiate with the head of one big company in each industry to set wage scales for the entire country. Because small manufacturers lacked the laborsaving machinery of their big competitors, small businesses would not be able to compete if they had to pay the same wages as the big corporations. Companies located in small towns or in traditionally low-wage regions would be forced to pay the same wages as manufacturers located in large urban areas of the Northeast and Midwest. Thus the leaders of both large

corporations and smaller companies worked together to amend the Wagner Act and weaken labor.

24. Anthony Leviero, "Wilson, Green Say Labor is Bending Toward Socialism," *New York Times*, January 22, 1947.

25. "Road to Socialism," *New York Times*, January 26, 1947.

26. As President Truman said, "If Communism is allowed to absorb the free nations, then we would be isolated from our sources of supply and detached from our friends. Then we would have to take defense measures which might really bankrupt our economy, and change our way of life so that we couldn't recognize it as American any longer." This would ultimately lead the United States to "become a garrison state, and to impose upon ourselves a system of centralized regimentation unlike anything we have ever known." Truman quoted in Melvyn Leffler, *A Preponderance of Power: National Security, the Truman Administration, and the Cold War* (Stanford: Stanford University Press, 1992), 13.

27. The anti-Communist section of the Taft-Hartley Act was adopted with relatively little fanfare. Lichtenstein, "Taft-Hartley: A Slave Labor Law?" *Catholic University Law Review* 47 (1988): 783.

28. David Lawrence, "The Real Communists," *Pulling Together: Bulletin of the Small Business Men's Association*, November 1947, enclosure.

29. Quote is from a resolution adopted by the Michigan CIO at its convention on March 13, 1948, quoted in Russell, *Out of the Jungle*, 157–58. The CIO's campaign was carried out nationwide, not just in Michigan. However, the Michigan CIO-PAC was at the forefront in implementing the pro–Democratic Party policies.

30. Julian G. McIntosh, Member of the Board of Commerce, "Let's Keep Enterprise Free," *Detroiter*, July 25, 1949.

31. Address by Herbert R. Dusendorf, Purchasing Agent, Nelson Company, Detroit before the 1950 Spring Meeting of the Central Supply Association, *Detroiter*, November 13, 1950.

32. Since its founding, the United States survived and thrived with a relatively weak federal government. In contrast, Europeans began developing powerful, centralized governments during the early modern period both to combat their enemies on the European continent and to assert control over their colonial possessions. As Charles Tilly has pointed out, war shaped the modern European state. European governments had to assemble large militaries, which required taxation, conscription, and bureaucracies. The United States, however, did not face any powerful external enemies for most of its history and did not participate in the scramble for overseas colonies until very late in the nineteenth century. As a result, the United States did not develop the sort of powerful, centralized states created in Europe. Charles Tilly quoted in Aaron Friedberg, *In the Shadow of the Garrison State: America's Anti-Statism and Its Cold War Grand Strategy* (Princeton: Princeton University Press, 2000), 3, 34.

33. Hayek, *Road to Serfdom*, 70.

34. Arnold quoted in David Reinhard, *The Republican Right Since 1945* (Lexington: University Press of Kentucky, 1983), 33.

35. Lasswell, quoted in Friedberg, *In the Shadow*, 57.

36. See Meg Jacobs, *Pocketbook Politics: Economic Citizenship in Twentieth-Century America* (Princeton, N.J.: Princeton University Press, 2007): 246–48. Housewives in particular urged the administration to institute controls. The Detroit Board of Commerce carried out a campaign to convince housewives that price controls would harm them. In a discussion before the Women's Town Meeting on radio station WWJ, Secretary of the Board Willis H. Hall asked, "Who pays for this fantastic price-control program? You the women of America pay for it! In fact you are paying for it twice— once when you pay high prices for the food for yourself and your family and again when you pay the taxes required to artificially prop up farm prices." Hall thus argued that price controls harmed the family economy and so should be opposed. Willis H. Hall, "Who Pays for Price Controls?" *Detroiter*, March 6, 1950, 5–6.

37. Zieger, *The CIO*, 294–295.

38. Meg Jacobs, *Pocketbook Politics: Economic Citizenship in Twentieth-Century America* (Princeton, NJ: Princeton University Press, 2005), 247–48; Lichtenstein, *Most Dangerous Man*, 281.

39. Zieger, *The CIO*, 295–97.

40. C. E. Wilson (GM), "The Camel's Nose Is under the Tent," *Detroiter*, October 22, 1951, 7.

41. Ernest R. Breech (Ford), speech to the Adcraft Club, *Detroiter*, September 1, 1952, 30.

42. "Paradox in Detroit," *Fortune*, January 1952, 41.

43. See testimony of Joseph L. Hartsell and John G. Weeks of the Hartsell Air Terminal Company and Bernard J. Teal, Teal Machine Products Company. Congress, Senate, Select Committee on Small Business, *Small-Business Problems in the Mobilization Program*, 82nd Cong., 1st sess., July 14 and 16, 1951, 3–22.

44. The snow-shoveling incident is discussed in "Ired by Cutbacks and Layoffs, Detroit Marches on Washington," *Newsweek*, January 7, 1952, 43.

45. This discussion of the Local 600-NNLC effort to stop decentralization draws heavily from Sugrue, *Origins*, 153–64.

46. Peter Shian, "All in the Name of Security," *Detroiter*, June 6, 1949, 1.

47. The Detroit Board of Commerce did engage in some gross red baiting during the Korean War. In his weekly column, Harvey Campbell regularly asked, "Under present union leadership, will American workers be able to produce implements to be used in any war against Russia?" When HUAC came to Detroit in 1952 to investigate Local 600, he wrote, "What a picture—suspect after suspect with Reuther's Union label—quivering cowards hiding the truth about their accomplices and overlords! Makes one sympathize with the millions of loyal American workers—Union captives, nauseated because of the banner they're forced to bear." However, the vast majority of business rhetoric on deindustrialization and Local 600 did not stress this theme. *Detroiter*, September 10, 1951, 3; February 25, 1952, 3.

48. "Of the 63 manufacturers who reported to the Detroit Metropolitan Area Planning Commission their reasons for moving from Detroit to other towns in this

area during the past 12 years, 70% gave high personal property taxes or high real estate taxes as their major reason while an additional 19% gave such taxes as a minor reason." John R. Stewart, "Detroit Grows its Own Industries," *Detroiter*, April 24, 1950.

49. Willis H. Hall, the Secretary-Manager of the Detroit Board of Commerce, presented a report to a Mayor's committee studying the impact of local taxes in 1957. According to his report, business inventories were assessed at 110 percent of value while real property was assessed at less than 50 percent of the current market price. As a result, businesses rather than homeowners bore the brunt of the city's tax burden. To support his claim that high taxes were driving industries from the city, Hall quoted from the 1956 City Plan Commission's Industrial Survey, prepared by the Manager of the Board's Industrial Department. According to this survey, the reason most often cited by manufacturers who planned on moving from Detroit was high taxes, followed by need for more manufacturing space, shortage of land for parking, labor problems, obsolete plants, and inadequacy of thoroughfares for moving goods and workers. "Hall's Report to Joseph Dodge," *Detroiter*, February 4, 1957, 6–7; "Review of City Plan Commission's 1956 Industrial Study," *Detroiter*, February 4, 1957, 8.

50. Nicholas Rini, "Board Backs Council's Concern over Tax Policy," *Detroiter*, November 15, 1954, 1.

51. Nicholas Rini, "Would You Rather Pay Than Protest?" *Detroiter*, March 14, 1955, 1.

52. Damon Stetson, "Michigan Warned by GM on Taxes," *New York Times*, April 29, 1957, 1.

53. "Government and Solicitations Chief Concern of Board of Commerce Members," *Detroiter*, June 9, 1958, 7.

54. Nicholas Rini, "Taxes on Business Up 1700% During Williams' Reign," *Detroiter*, September 7, 1959, 1.

55. Tyrone Gillespie, assistant to the president of Dow Chemical Co., "Will Governor Williams's Tax Proposals Further Injure Michigan?" *Detroiter*, March 30, 1959, 6–7. In December 1958, Michigan lacked sufficient money to meet the state's payroll. In response, a special legislative committee studied the state's tax structure and used the recommendations of a special Citizens' Advisory Committee. Three members of the citizens' committee, including Gillespie, disagreed with the committee's majority report and wrote their own minority dissent.

56. Nicholas Rini, "Fair Deal for Business is Key to New Jobs," *Detroiter*, September 21, 1959, 1.

57. John R. Stewart, "Detroit Worker Holds Top Wage Position," *Detroiter*, July 11, 1949, 1.

58. General Motors was one of a number of corporations that turned to corporate welfare to try to tie workers more closely to their employers. These companies hoped that their private welfare system would weaken worker reliance on the union and

the state. Fones-Wolf, *Selling Free Enterprise*, 86; Lichtenstein, *Most Dangerous Man*, 278–88, 285–86.

59. Lichtenstein, *Most Dangerous Man*, 280–81.

60. Lichtenstein, *Most Dangerous Man*, 314–315.

61. Reuther, quoted in Lichtenstein, *Most Dangerous Man*, 282, 284.

62. GM executives decided that they had to protect the interests of the company, even if it meant alienating their fellow businessmen. They argued that, in this case, "what was good for GM . . . might not be so good for industry in general." In letters to Donaldson Brown, Alfred Sloan wrote that agreements made between GM or Ford and the UAW "have had a dominating influence in forcing others to make similar agreements, whether they are in an economic position to do so or not. Personally, I think this is most unfortunate, but I do not know what we can do about it." Sloan argued that "We have to do the best thing we can for ourselves because that is what we are in business for." Personal letters from Alfred Sloan to Donaldson Brown, September 19, 1955, and December 15, 1955, Donaldson Brown Collection, Box 1, Hagley Museum.

63. Unnamed Detroit businessman quoted in "A Problem for GM's Policymakers" *Business Week*, February 13, 1954, 68.

64. "Reuther's GAW-ful Fraud," Earl Harding, Vice President, National Economic Council Inc., *Economic Council Letter*, September 1, 1955, in Donaldson Brown Collection, Box 1, Hagley.

65. "What the National Economic Council Is—And Is Not," Economic Council Papers, July 15, 1950, reprinted in Economic Council Letter, August 15, 1955, Donaldson Brown Collection, Box 1, Hagley Museum.

66. "GAW and Small Business," *Pulling Together: Bulletin of the Small Business Men's Association*, May 1955, 1.

67. Before the mid-1950s, the Big Three relied heavily on smaller firms for parts and equipment. In 1941, one auto firm regularly used twelve thousand suppliers to manufacture its cars. During World War II, fifty-six cents out of every dollar earned by auto companies for war orders went to either vendors or subcontractors. Of these, 63 percent were small businesses that employed fewer than five hundred employees. "Small Businesses Share Defense Jobs," *Detroiter*, April 23, 1951, 6; Sugrue, *Origins*, 137–38.

68. Lichtenstein, *State of the Union*, 98–99.

69. *Detroiter*, April 2, 1951, 4.

70. Harvey Campbell, "Where is Detroit Going?" *Detroiter*, October 18, 1948, 5. Biographical information about Campbell appears in "Looking to the Future: Our Second Century," *Detroiter*, June 1, 2003, 1.

71. Harvey Campbell, "What Goes on Here" *Detroiter*, November 15, 1948, 3.

72. This was Thomas Paine's definition of the word "republic." M. J. Heale, *American Anticommunism: Combatting the Enemy Within* (Baltimore: Johns Hopkins University Press, 1990), 10.

73. Campbell, "What Goes on Here," 3.

74. *Ibid.*

75. Mike Davis, *Prisoners of the American Dream: Politics and Economy in the History of the U.S. Working Class* (London: Verso, 1986), 122.

76. The auto industry was particularly hard hit by the 1957–58 recession. As a result, Detroit suffered far higher unemployment than did the rest of the country. While national unemployment averaged 6.7 percent, 15.1 percent of the Detroit labor force was out of work. "Recession in Detroit: Chronic Aches Hurt Badly in Hard Times," *Time*, April 14, 1958, 18. Employment in nonautomotive manufacturing in the metropolitan area remained fairly steady during the downturn. However, the number of jobs in the automotive and equipment industry and in industries closely tied to auto production fell sharply. In January 1957, employment declined by sixty-two thousand from its 1956 average. Of these lost jobs, forty-nine thousand were in automobile production and fourteen thousand were in automotive-related industries. *Detroiter*, January 14, 1957, 1. The pattern continued one year later. See *Detroiter*, February 10, 1958, 1.

77. Fund raising letter from I. H. Latimer, Executive Vice-Chairman of the Illinois Right to Work Committee, 1957, Latimer Collection, Box 58, Fund Raising: RTW Committee: 1957 Folder, Chicago Historical Society, Chicago; Goldwater quote from Rick Perlstein, *Before the Storm: Barry Goldwater and the Unmaking of the American Consensus* (New York: Hill and Wang, 2001), 33.

78. After the 1956 election, Eisenhower declared that "gradually expanding federal government" was the "price of rapidly expanding national growth." For both the Eisenhower quote and a discussion of Manion, see Perlstein, *Before the Storm*, 16.

79. Manion quote in Perlstein, *Before the Storm*, 32.

80. *New York Times*, March 2, 1957. Manion was also at the forefront of an effort to amend Taft-Hartley in order to return control over local strikes to states rather than have that control rest with the federal government. Manion complained, "Federal intervention has destroyed the power of the States to prevent or to minimize strikes, picketing, boycotts and lockouts." In addition, Manion sought to protect small business, which was in a virtual no-man's-land in labor law as a result of Supreme Court and NLRB decisions. The Supreme Court had ruled that state labor laws were invalid if they dealt with problems covered by the Taft-Hartley Act. The National Labor Relations Board had ruled that it would refrain from exercising jurisdiction in cases involving businesses whose direct interstate volume was less than $500,000 annually, or whose total interstate volume is less than 1 million. As a result, small businesses often found themselves with no recourse and no forum with which to obtain relief. Because NLRB jurisdiction had been asserted, state law did not apply, but because the NLRB had declined to exercise jurisdiction, the federal board would take no action. As a result of these decisions, small businesses could not obtain relief at either the state or federal level. 1954 statement, Manion Collection, Box 2, Folder 2–10, Chicago Historical Society, Chicago.

81. Shermer, "Origins," 697–699.

82. Perlstein, *Before the Storm*, 28, 37.

83. *New York Times*, March 17, 1957; A. H. Raskin, "Labor Faces Renewed Right-to-Work Drive," *New York Times*, September 15, 1957. Quote is from an unnamed supporter.

84. Damon Stetson, "Michigan Beset by Varied Woes," *New York Times*, June 9, 1957.

85. James M. Haswell, "McClellan Runs UAW Quiz," *Detroit Free Press*, January 9, 1958.

86. Tom Nicholson, "Union Demands Pay Hike, Too," *Detroit Free Press*, January 14, 1958.

87. "How Big Three See UAW Proposal," *Detroit Free Press*, January 14, 1958; "Breech Lays it on the Line," *Detroit Free Press*, January 25, 1958.

88. "Brow-Raising Bid By the Wayne GOP," *Detroit Free Press*, January 20, 1958.

89. In attendance were Harlow Curtice of GM, Sherrod Skinner, GM's vice president in charge of accessories, and Allen Merrill, assistant to the president of Ford, and former GM vice president Don Ahrens. Will Muller, "'Stop Reuther' Plea Given State GOP" *Detroit News*, January 21, 1958; *Time*, February 3, 1958, 11; Perlstein, *Before the Storm*, 37–38.

90. Will Muller, "'Stop Reuther' Plea Given State GOP" *Detroit News*, January 21, 1958; "Recession in Detroit" *Time*, April 14, 1958, 18.

91. Creighton quoted in Owen C. Deatrick, "Williams Blasted by Legislator," *Detroit Free Press*, January 11, 1958; Hutchinson quoted in Owen C. Deatrick, "GOP Says Williams Is Failure," *Detroit Free Press*, January 12, 1958; Republican party quote from "Michigan Economic Climate Harms Job Growth" Michigan Republican Plain Talk, August 1958, 1; Goldwater quote from *New York Times*, March 30, 1958.

92. Shermer, "Origins," 707.

93. "Michigan Democrats Aided by Slump, Survey Shows" *New York Times*, October 25, 1958.

94. Damon Stetson, "Democrats Gain Michigan Sweep," *New York Times*, November 6, 1958.

CONCLUSION

1. Allitt, *Conservatives*, 159.

2. Michael Cain, "The 'Key' to Continuing the 'Catholic Connection' in Fighting the 'Evil Empire!'" *Daily Catholic*, November 5–7, 1999, vol. 10, no. 202.

3. Richard Gid Powers, *Not Without Honor: The History of American Anticommunism* (New York: Free Press, 1995), 425.

WORKS CITED

Archival Collections

AAD   Archives of the Archdiocese of Detroit, Detroit, Michigan
    Edward Mooney Collection
    Chancery Collection
    Parish Collection, Parishes Outside of Detroit to 1958
    Parish Collections:
        St. Rose of Lima
        St. Albertus
        St. Anthony
        St. Johns
        St. Margaret Mary
ALUA   Archives of Labor and Urban Affairs, Walter P. Reuther Library,
Wayne State University, Detroit, Michigan
    Association of Catholic Trade Unionists, (ACTU), Detroit
    Olive Beasley Collection
    Civil Rights Congress of Michigan
    Gloucester Current Collection
    George Edwards Collection
    Richard Frankensteen Collection
    Charles Hill Collection
    Walter P. Reuther Collection
    UAW-IEB Collection
AWHS   Archives of the Wisconsin Historical Society, University
of Wisconsin, Madison
    American Federation of Labor Records
CHS   Chicago Historical Society, Chicago, Illinois
    Ira Latimer Papers
    Clarence Manion Papers

DPL   Burton Historical Collection, Detroit Public Library
            Detroit Archives—Mayor's Papers, 1947–56
            Malcolm Dade Papers
            Detroit Commission on Community Relations Collection
Hagley Hagley Museum and Library, Wilmington, Delaware
            F. Donaldson Brown Collection
            J. Howard Pew Collection
LC   Manuscript Division, Library of Congress, Washington, D.C.
            National Association for the Advancement of Colored People
            (NAACP) Papers
MHC   Michigan Historical Collections, Bentley Library, University
        of Michigan, Ann Arbor
            Rensis Likert Papers

Periodicals

Business Week
Brightmoor Journal
Detroit Free Press
Detroit Labor News
Detroit News
Detroiter
Ford Facts
Fortune
Labor Action
Michigan Catholic
Michigan Chronicle
New York Times
Newsweek
Pittsburgh Courier, Detroit Edition
Pulling Together: Bulletin of the Small Business Men's Association
Redford Record
Wage Earner

Published Sources

Annual Report of General Motors Corporation. Detroit, Michigan: General Motors Corporation, 1944.
Annual Report of General Motors Corporation. Detroit, Michigan: General Motors Corporation, 1945.
Annual Report of General Motors Corporation. Detroit, Michigan: General Motors Corporation, 1946.
Detroit Area Study. *A Social Profile of Detroit, 1953: A Report of the Detroit Area Study of the University of Michigan.* Ann Arbor: University of Michigan, 1954.

Detroit Area Study. *A Social Profile of Detroit, 1956: A Report of the Detroit Area Study of the University of Michigan*. Ann Arbor: University of Michigan, 1957.

Gallup, George H. *The Gallup Poll: Public Opinion 1935–1971*. Wilmington, Del.: Scholarly Resources, 1971.

Kornhauser, Arthur. *Detroit as the People See It*. Detroit: Wayne University Press, 1952.

Leo XIII. *Rerum Novarum: Encyclical Letter of Pope Leo XIII on the Condition of the Working Classes*. London: Catholic Truth Society, 1983.

Miller, L. G. "The Rosary Next Door." *Perpetual Help*, August 1950.

Pius XI, *Quadragesimo Anno (The Fortieth Year): On Reconstruction of the Social Order*. Chicago: Outline Press, 1947.

Pius XI. *Encyclical Letter of Pope Pius XI on Atheistic Communism*. Boston: St. Paul Editions, 1937.

Schorn, Nicholas. "Why the Block Rosary." *Our Lady of the Cape*, February 1952, 7–10.

U.S. Bureau of the Census. *Census of the Population, 1950, Volume II, Characteristics of the Population, Part 22, Michigan*. Washington, D.C.: GPO, 1952.

U.S. Bureau of the Census. *Census of the Population, 1950, Vol. III, Census Tract Statistics, Chapter 17*. Washington, D.C.: GPO, 1952.

U.S. Congress. House. Committee on Un-American Activities. *Communism in the Detroit Area: Hearings before the Committee on Un-American Activities, House of Representatives*. 82nd Cong., 2nd. sess., February 25–29, 1952.

U.S. Congress. House. Special Committee on Post-War Economic Policy and Planning. *Post-War Economic Policy and Planning Part 1: Contract Termination and Related Matters*. 78th Cong., 2nd Sess., March 22, 1944.

U.S. Congress. Senate. Select Committee on Small Business. *Small-Business Problems in the Mobilization Program*. 82nd Cong., 1st sess., 14 and 16 July, 1951.

Secondary Sources

Allitt, Patrick. *Catholic Intellectuals and Conservative Politics in America, 1950–1985*. Ithaca, N.Y: Cornell University Press, 1993.

———. *The Conservatives: Ideas and Personalities throughout American History*. New Haven, Conn.: Yale University Press, 2009.

Arnesen, Eric. "No 'Graver Danger': Black Anticommunism, the Communist Party, and the Race Question." *Labor: Studies in Working-Class History of the Americas* 3 (Winter 2006): 13–52.

Balogh, Brian. *Chain Reaction: Expert Debate and Public Participation In American Commercial Nuclear Power, 1945–1975*. Cambridge: Cambridge University Press, 1991.

Baskin, Alex. "The Ford Hunger March—1932." *Labor History* 13, no. 3: 331–60.

Berg, Manfred. "Black Civil Rights and Liberal Anticommunism: The NAACP in the Early Cold War." *Journal of American History*, June 2007: 75–96.

Blackbourn, David. *Marpingen: Apparitions of the Virgin Mary in a Nineteenth-Century German Village*. New York: Vintage, 1993.

Biondi, Martha. *To Stand and Fight: The Struggle for Civil Rights in Postwar New York City.* Cambridge: Harvard University Press, 2003.

Boyle, Kevin. *The UAW and the Heyday of American Liberalism, 1945–1968.* Ithaca, N.Y.: Cornell University Press, 1995.

Brinkley, Alan. *The End of Reform: New Deal Liberalism in Recession and War.* New York: Vintage, 1995.

———. *Liberalism and its Discontents.* Cambridge: Harvard University Press, 1998.

———. "The Problem of American Conservatism." *American Historical Review* 99 no. 2 (April, 1994): 409–29.

———. *Voices of Protest: Huey Long, Father Coughlin, and the Great Depression.* New York: Knopf, 1982.

Buffa, Dudley W. *Union Power and American Democracy: The UAW and the Democratic Party, 1935–72.* Ann Arbor: University of Michigan Press, 1984.

Calazza, John. "American Conservatism and the Catholic Church." *Modern Age,* Winter 2010: 14–24.

Capeci, Jr., Dominic, and Martha Wilkerson. *Layered Violence: The Detroit Rioters of 1943.* Jackson, Miss.: University Press of Mississippi, 1991.

Carter, Dan T. *The Politics of Rage: George Wallace, the Origins of the New Conservatism, and the Transformation of American Politics.* New York: Simon & Schuster, 1995.

Christian, William A. *Visionaries: The Spanish Republic and the Reign of Christ.* Berkeley: University of California Press, 1996.

Conot, Robert. *American Odyssey: A History of a Great City.* Detroit: Wayne State University, 1986.

Critchlow, Donald T. *Phyllis Schlafly and Grassroots Conservatism: A Woman's Crusade.* Princeton, N.J.: Princeton University Press, 2005.

Davis, Mike. *Prisoners of the American Dream: Politics and Economy in the History of the U.S. Working Class.* London: Verso, 1986.

Dolan, Jay. *The American Catholic Experience: A History from Colonial Times to the Present.* Notre Dame, Ind.: University of Notre Dame Press, 1992.

DuBois, W. E. B. *The Autobiography of W. E. B. DuBois.* New York: International, 1968.

Edsall, Thomas Byrne, and Mary D. Edsall. *Chain Reaction: The Impact of Race, Rights, and Taxes on American Politics.* New York: Norton, 1991.

Farley, Reynolds, Sheldon Danziger, and Harry H. Holzer. *Detroit Divided: A Volume in the Multi-City Study of Urban Inequality.* New York: Sage, 2000.

Ferguson, Thomas. "From Normalcy to New Deal: Industrial Structure, Party Competition, and American Public Policy in the Great Depression." *International Organization,* Winter 1984: 41–94.

Fones-Wolf, Elizabeth. *Selling Free Enterprise: The Business Assault on Labor and Liberalism, 1945–1960.* Urbana: University of Illinois Press, 1994.

Fraser, Steven. *Labor Will Rule: Sidney Hillman and the Rise of American Labor.* New York: Free Press, 1991.

Friedberg, Aaron. *In the Shadow of the Garrison State: America's Anti-Statism and Its Cold War Grand Strategy*. Princeton: Princeton University Press, 2000.

Gerstle, Gary. *American Crucible: Race and Nation in the Twentieth Century*. Princeton, N.J.: Princeton University Press, 2001.

———. "Race and the Myth of the Liberal Consensus." *Journal of American History* 82, no. 2 (September 1995): 579–86.

Griffith, Robert. "Forging America's Postwar Order: Domestic Politics and Political Economy in the Age of Truman." In *The Truman Presidency*, edited by Michael J. Lacey, 57–88. New York: Cambridge University Press, 1991.

Griffith, Robert, and Athan Theoharis, eds. *The Specter: Original Essays on the Cold War and the Origins of McCarthyism*. New York: New Viewpoints, 1974.

Halpern, Martin. "'I'm Fighting for Freedom': Coleman Young, HUAC, and the Detroit African American Community," *Journal of American Ethnic History* 17, no.1 (1997): 19–38.

———. *UAW Politics in the Cold War Era*. Albany: State University of New York Press, 1988.

———. *Unions, Radicals, and Democratic Presidents: Seeking Social Change in the Twentieth Century*. Westport: Praeger, 2003.

Harris, Howell. *The Right to Manage: Industrial Relations Policies of American Business in the 1940s*. Madison: University of Wisconsin Press, 1982.

Heale, M. J. *American Anticommunism: Combatting the Enemy Within*. Baltimore, Md.: Johns Hopkins University Press, 1990.

———. *McCarthy's Americans: Red Scare Politics in State and Nation, 1935–1965*. Athens: University of Georgia Press, 1998.

———. "The Triumph of Liberalism? Red Scare Politics in Michigan, 1938–1954." *Proceedings of the American Philosophical Society*, March 1995: 44–66.

Henrickson, Wilma Wood. *Detroit Perspectives: Crossroads and Turning Points*. Detroit: Wayne State University Press, 1991.

Hirsch, Arnold. *Making the Second Ghetto: Race and Housing in Chicago, 1940–1960*. New York: Cambridge University Press, 1983.

Horne, Gerald. *Black and Red: W. E. B. DuBois and the Afro-American Response to the Cold War, 1944–1963*. Albany: State University of New York Press, 1986.

Huff, Peter A. *Allen Tate and the Catholic Revival: Trace of the Fugitive Gods*. New York : Paulist Press, 1996.

Isserman, Maurice. *Which Side Where You On? The American Communist Party during the Second World War*. Middletown, Conn.: Wesleyan University Press, 1982.

Jackson, Kenneth. *Crabgrass Frontier: The Suburbanization of the United States*. New York: Oxford University Press, 1985.

Jackson, Walter. *Gunnar Myrdal and America's Conscience*. Chapel Hill: University of North Carolina Press, 1990.

Jacobs, Meg. "'How About Some Meat?': The Office of Price Administration, Consumption Politics, and State Building from the Bottom Up, 1941–1946," *Journal of American History* 84, no. 3 (December 1997): 910–41.

————. *Pocketbook Politics: Economic Citizenship in Twentieth-Century America.* Princeton, N.J.: Princeton University Press, 2005.

Johnson, Kathryn A. "The Home is a Little Church: Gender, Culture, and Authority in American Catholicism, 1940–1962." PhD diss., University of Pennsylvania, 1997.

Judis, John. *William F. Buckley, Jr.: Patron Saint of the Conservatives.* New York: Simon & Schuster, 2001.

Keeran, Roger. *The Communist Party and the Auto Workers Unions.* Bloomington: Indiana University Press, 1980.

Keller, Morton. "The New Deal: A New Look," *Polity,* Summer 1999: 660.

Kennedy, David M. *Freedom from Fear: The American People in Depression and War, 1929–1945.* New York: Oxford University Press, 1999.

Kersten, Andrew E. *Labor's Home Front: The American Federation of Labor During World War II.* New York: New York University Press, 2006.

Klehr, Harvey. *The Heyday of American Communism: The Depression Decade.* New York: Basic, 1984.

Klug, Thomas A. "Labor Market Politics in Detroit: The Curious Case of the 'Spolansky Act' of 1931." *Michigan Historical Review* 14, no. 1 (Spring, 1988): 1–32.

Kornhauser, Arthur. *Detroit as the People See It: A Survey of Attitudes in an Industrial City.* Detroit: Wayne University Press, 1952.

Lassiter, Matthew D. *The Silent Majority: Suburban Politics in the Sunbelt South.* Princeton, N.J.: Princeton University Press, 2007.

Lee, Alfred McClung, and Norman Daymond Humphrey. "The Interracial Committee of the City of Detroit: A Case History." *Journal of Educational Sociology* 19 (January 1946): 278–88.

Leff, Mark. "The Politics of Sacrifice on the American Home Front in World War II." *Journal of American History,* March 1991: 1296–318.

Leffler, Melvyn. *A Preponderance of Power: National Security, the Truman Administration, and the Cold War.* Stanford: Stanford University Press, 1992.

Lenski, Gerhard. *The Religious Factor: A Sociological Study of Religion's Impact on Politics, Economics, And Family Life.* Garden City, N.Y.: Doubleday, 1961.

Levenstein, Harvey. *Communism, Anticommunism and the CIO.* Westport, Conn.: Greenwood, 1981 [Chapter 1, note 9].

Lewis, Anders Geoffery. "Labor's Cold War: The AFL and Liberal Anticommunism." PhD diss., University of Florida, 2000.

Lewis-Colman, David M. *Race against Liberalism: Black Workers and the UAW in Detroit.* Chicago: University of Illinois Press, 2008.

Lichtenstein, Nelson. *Labor's War at Home: The CIO in World War II.* Philadelphia: Temple University Press, 2003.

————. "Life at the Rouge: A Cycle of Workers' Control." In *Life and Labor: Dimensions of American Working Class History,* edited by Charles Stephenson and Robert Asher, 237–59. Albany: SUNY Press, 1986.

————. *The Most Dangerous Man in Detroit: Walter Reuther and the Fate of American Labor.* New York: Basic, 1995.

———. *State of the Union: A Century of American Labor*. Princeton, N.J.: Princeton University Press, 2002.

———. "Taft-Hartley: A Slave Labor Law?" *Catholic University Law Review* 47 (1988): 766–89.

Lichtman, Allan J. *White Protestant Nation: The Rise of the American Conservative Movement*. New York: Atlantic Monthly Press, 2008, 2.

Lifka, Thomas. *The Concept "Totalitarianism" and American Foreign Policy, 1933–1949*. New York: Garland, 1988.

Marable, Manning. *Race, Reform, and Rebellion: The Second Reconstruction in Black America, 1945–1990*. Jackson: University of Mississippi Press, 1991.

May, Elaine Tyler. *Homeward Bound: American Families in the Cold War Era*. New York: Basic, 1990.

McGirr, Lisa. *Suburban Warriors: The Origins of the New American Right*. Princeton, N.J.: Princeton University Press, 2001.

McGreevey, John. *Parish Boundaries: The Catholic Encounter with Race in the 20th Century Urban North*. Chicago: University of Chicago Press, 1996.

McQuaid, Kim. *Uneasy Partners: Big Business in American Politics, 1945–1990*. Baltimore, Md.: Johns Hopkins Press, 1994.

Meier, August, and Rudwick, Elliott. *Black Detroit and the Rise of the UAW*. New York: Oxford University Press, 1979.

Nowak, Margaret Collingwood. *Two Who Were There: A Biography of Stanley Nowak*. Detroit: Wayne State University Press, 1989.

Orsi, Robert. "Abundant History: Marian Apparitions as Alternative Modernity." *Historically Speaking*, September/October 2008: 12–16.

———. *The Madonna of 115th Street: Faith and Community in Italian Harlem*. New Haven, Conn.: Yale University Press, 2002.

———. *Thank You, St. Jude: Women's Devotion to the Patron Saint of Lost Causes*. New Haven, Conn.: Yale University Press, 1996.

Perlstein, Rick. *Before the Storm: Barry Goldwater and the Unmaking of the American Consensus*. New York: Hill and Wang, 2001.

Phillips-Fein, Kim. *Invisible Hands: The Making of the Conservative Movement from the New Deal to Reagan*. New York: Norton, 2009.

Powers, Richard Gid. *Not Without Honor: The History of American Anticommunism*. New York: Free Press, 1995.

Reinhard, David. *The Republican Right Since 1945*. Lexington: University Press of Kentucky, 1983.

Ribuffo, Leo. "Conservatism and American Politics." *Journal of the Historical Society* 3, no. 2 (Spring 2003): 163–75.

Rosenof, Theodore. "Freedom, Planning and Totalitarianism: The Reception of F. A. Hayek's *Road to Serfdom*." *Canadian Review of American Studies*, Fall 1974: 49–165.

Rosswurm, Steve. *The CIO's Left-Led Unions*. New Brunswick, N.J.: Rutgers University Press, 1992.

Russell, Thaddeus. *Out of the Jungle: Jimmy Hoffa and the Remaking of the American Working Class*. New York: Knopf, 2001.

Scott, Daryl. *Contempt and Pity: Social Policy and the Image of the Damaged Black Psyche, 1880–1960*. Chapel Hill: University of North Carolina Press, 1997.

Selcraig, James Truett. *The Red Scare in the Midwest, 1945–1955: A State and Local Study*. UMI Research, 1982.

Shermer, Elizabeth Tandy. "Origins of the Conservative Ascendancy: Barry Goldwater's Early Senate Career and the De-legitimization of Organized Labor." *Journal of American History*, December 2008: 678–709.

Smith, Carl O., and Stephen B. Sarasohn. "Hate Propaganda in Detroit." *Public Opinion Quarterly*, Spring 1946: 24–52.

Sugrue, Thomas. *The Origins of the Urban Crisis: Race and Inequality in Postwar Detroit*. Princeton, N.J.: Princeton University Press, 1996.

Tentler, Leslie. *Seasons of Grace: A History of the Catholic Archdiocese of Detroit*. Detroit: Wayne State University Press, 1990.

Thompson, Heather Ann. *Whose Detroit: Politics, Labor and Race in a Modern American City*. Ithaca, N.Y.: Cornell University Press, 2001.

Turrini, Joseph. "Phooie on Louie: African American Detroit and the Election of Jerry Cavanagh." *Michigan History*, November/December 1999, 11–17.

Warner, Marina. *Alone of All Her Sex: The Myth and the Cult of the Virgin Mary*. New York: Vintage, 1983.

Weiss, Nancy J. *Farewell to the Party of Lincoln: Black Politics in the Age of FDR*. Princeton, N.J.: Princeton University Press, 1983.

Widick, B. J. *Detroit: City of Race and Class Violence*. Detroit: Wayne State University Press, 1989.

Wilkins, Roy. *Standing Fast: The Autobiography of Roy Wilkins*. New York: Da Capo, 1994.

Workman, Andrew. "Manufacturing Power: The Organizational Revival of the National Association of Manufacturers, 1941–1945." *Business History Review* 72 (Summer 1998): 279–317.

Zelizer, Julian E. "Rethinking the History of American Conservatism." *Reviews in American History* 38, no. 2 (2010): 367–92.

Zieger, Robert H. *The CIO: 1933–1955*. Chapel Hill: University of North Carolina Press, 1995.

Zimdars-Swartz, Sandra L. *Encountering Mary: From LaSalette to Medjugorje*. Princeton: Princeton University Press, 1991.

Zunz, Olivier. *The Changing Face of Inequality: Urbanization, Industrial Development, and Immigrants in Detroit, 1880–1920*. Chicago: University of Chicago Press, 1982.

INDEX

Addes, George, 33, 51–52

affirmative action programs, 2–3

AFL (American Federation of Labor): Cold War–era antilabor laws and anti-Communist stance, 35–36; Detroit Building Trades Unions, 26; garbage workers strike position, 43; loyalty oath position, 41–42; postwar attacks on CIO, 26, 131n34; postwar liberal agenda, 132n44; pre-war anti-Communism overview, 16–18; UAW-AFL, 14

African Americans: Communist Party support for civil rights struggles of 1930s and 1940s, 11–12; Detroit racial issues overview, 120; liberal opposition to Communism, 56–59, 139–40n36; postwar fair employment struggle, 68–74; race riots of 1943, 52–53; racial violence of 1952, 47; racist reaction to black population explosion, 48–49; United Public Workers of America (UPWA-CIO), 32–33; World War II migration into Detroit, 20–23, 48, 53. See also black liberals; civil rights movement

Ahrens, Don, 115

Allis Chalmers strike, 17

American Federation of State County and Municipal Employees (AFSC&ME-AFL), 42

Americans for Democratic Action (ADA), 35

American Slav Congress, 81–82

anti-Communism: American Federation of Labor (AFL) in 1930s, 16–18; as anachronism, 123; anti-Semitism connection, 78, 79; black liberals, 47, 54, 64–65, 72–73, 137n3, 147n78; business elite capitalist authority context, 12, 13; business overview, 121; Catholic devotions, 1, 83–91, 146–47n31, 147n34, 147–48n36, 148n37, 149n48; Catholicism connection, 76–77, 91–92, 121–22; Catholic media, 146n28; Catholic traditionalism, 83–89; city government-Communism perception, 40; civil rights organizations alliance, 54; Communist Party demonstrations of 1930s, 13; conservatism relationship, 44–45; Detroit Citizens Committee for Equal Employment Opportunities, 70–71; Eastern European ethnic groups, 80–83; election of 1946, 30–31; Korean War, 42–43; liberal New Deal themes opposition, 126n15; Nazi-Soviet pact, 17; 1930s roots, 12–16; overviews, 5–6, 7, 121–23; postwar legislation, 34; pre-war and postwar demographics, 9–10; red-baiting of 1945 mayoral election, 24–25; red scare of 1949, 38–42; subversive investigation of 1930, 12–13; UAW strikes against military production, 17–18; as unifying element of popular conservatism, 2

anti-government politics, 125–26n12

anti-secularism, 86–89

anti-Semitism, 78, 79

Arnesen, Eric, 57

Arnold, Wat, 103

COLLEEN DOODY is an assistant professor of history at DePaul University.

THE WORKING CLASS IN AMERICAN HISTORY

The University of Illinois Press
is a founding member of the
Association of American University Presses.

University of Illinois Press
1325 South Oak Street
Champaign, IL 61820-6903
www.press.uillinois.edu